CW00860216

Miracles of Choice

Miracles of Choice

Discovering Forgotten Gifts of Free Will

Lorelai I. Dali

Dali, Lorelai I. *Miracles of Choice.*

FIRST EDITION

ISBN 978-1-4717-2602-6

CONTENTS

ACKNOWLEDGMENTS

I consider myself to be at very exciting part of my Life Journey. I have been through experiences of various kinds. I have faced numerous challenges. I have been blessed with millions of moments of happiness, and cried through millions of moments of sadness. I have fought, I have won and I have surrendered. Sometimes I even run away and hid my head in the sand. It seems like all of the experiences have been my Elementary School classes and I feel that I have graduated with honors. Not because I possessed extensive knowledge, but because I have learned something from each of the moments of my life and I came through on the other side stronger than ever, despite the odds.

And who were my teachers? Each and every person that I have ever met. Therefore I would like to send the thoughts of deepest gratitude to all of the people who loved me, hated me, looked up to me, praised me, scolded me, criticized me, made me laugh, made me cry, got mad at me, ignored me, mistreated me, supported me, listened to me, gave me an advice, hugged me, pushed me away, dug holes under me, gave me a helping hand or just passed through my life. You were all significant in the ways I sometimes don't even understand. So thank you from the bottom of my heart.

Most of all I would like to send my love to my closest family, my daughter Marta and my partner Konrad, who pushed me towards reaching my dreams, gave me time, space and love when I needed it the most, and stood by me in the moments of doubt. And big thank you to my parents, who were my first teachers and through mysterious ways showed me who I wanted to become.

With this book I am entering my life's High School and I couldn't be more excited!

Love to you all!

Lorelai I. Dali

Miracles of Choice

Miracle of Retrospection

"What brought me here?"

Mirjam was sitting on a rocky Irish beach on a first warm day that summer, with that question echoing repeatedly in her mind.

"What brought me here?"

Out of the thousands of beaches in hundreds of cities around the world, she was sitting on this one. A few years ago, she didn't even know this beach existed. She never thought of Ireland, except when walking by an Irish pub on a busy street of a laid back Florida town. And now - here she was.

Mirjam hasn't had a boring life. She was only thirty and had already lived in three different countries. She had ten different jobs in her adult life, ranging from accounting to cleaning houses and designing jewelry. Numerous relationships made her aware of how different people were, how culture, religion and family dynamics affected one's abilities to reach for their dreams or drown in the sea of unhappiness and despair. She wasn't a stranger to self-development, reading psychological, self-help and esoteric books since she was a teenager. She even explored witchcraft and energy healing and heard of the thing called the 'Law of Attraction', although she never fully understood the underlying processes of these mystical arts. She was always searching, knowing that she was getting closer to finding the meaning of life, but now she was baffled by this simple question.

"What brought me here?"

She kept thinking, searching the puzzles of knowledge that she had gained from numerous sources and kept stored in the labyrinths of her inner mind. What brought her here? Was it many small accidents that she had no control over? Or maybe fate that was written in heavenly scriptures long before she was even born? Or maybe someone else made her do it?

The puzzles didn't make any sense, they just wouldn't form any picture. So she stopped thinking and allowed herself to just be. And then she knew.

"It was me," she said, "I brought myself to this exact point in space and time. I did it with the choices I made."

And she knew it wasn't just about deciding whether she lived in this country or another, if she worked or played, if she stayed or if she left. Those were obviously her choices, although she wasn't always clear about her motivations just yet. But now she knew that she also made millions of little choices every day of what she thought, how she acted or reacted, what she said, and how she felt about herself and the world. These little choices that she never really realized she was making were the ones affecting her life the most.

PROLOGUE

We don't even realize it, but at each moment of our lives we make choices. From the moment we are born to the moment we die - we choose. As babies, we choose which games we like to play, which toys we like better than the others, which foods we eat with appetite. When we grow a bit older, we choose what subjects interest us more - music, drawing, or maybe sports? Later - what career path do we take? Where do we want to live? Who do we want to spend the rest of our lives with? Those are the big ones, the "obvious" choices.

But there are also the smaller, what seems less noticeable choices - do we wake up with the smile on our faces or do we see each day as a never-ending unpleasant errand? Do we see the glass half full or half empty? Do we listen to our hearts or do we please others? Do we choose to choose or let others choose for us? Even refusing to make choice is a choice.

You'll probably hear an inner voice of disagreement now: *"How can you say that I chose to be a shy person? I was born this way, this is who I am!"* I will answer: you choose how to look at the world and how you act in it. Maybe you are more sensitive than others, maybe you were shy when you were a child, but you choose to stay shy. *You* make yourself be this way.

You might say: *"I had a terrible childhood. This affected me so much that I cannot help but to act in a certain way."* I will answer: yes, this was tragic, I'm sure if affected you deeply. But *you* choose to let the past have such strong hold on you to this day. You can choose to hold on to it or to let go.

You might add: *"My boss is such a bad person, he makes me so angry!"* I will answer: your boss might be a bad person, but *you* choose how you feel about him. Nobody can make you feel anything you don't want to feel.

Your way of looking at your life and experiencing this world is YOUR choice. Things may happen, but you choose whether they affect you and how you react to them.

The point of this book is to remind you of your own inner power. You are not a helpless victim of life's circumstances. You create your life's circumstances. You don't have to let the whims of others push you in directions that make you unhappy. You decide which routes to take. You are not restricted to the beliefs that you learned in your childhood. You choose how you feel about yourself and what you think about the world.

I want to show you the way to find this power within and to take back the control of your life.

It is YOUR life, isn't it?

So live it YOUR way!

"Happiness depends upon ourselves."
~ Aristotle ~

Miracle of Respecting Yourself

Mirjam always wanted to know the reason for her existence. When she was growing up, she had no help from her parents in understanding this mysterious subject. They were wealth driven people, born into poverty, so material security was what mattered to them the most. They ran their own business, always talking about how important it was to have high life standard. They wanted to show their neighbors and friends how big and important they were, not realizing they were only covering their own insecurities with material possessions.

Mirjam's mother wanted her to gain a "good education" so she sent her to high profile private school and signed her up for so many after-school programs that Mirjam never had time to figure out what she really liked to do. She really enjoyed painting, but she could only do it in hiding. Painting was not a respected profession, according to her parents. She was told that she needed to study and learn and although she did that from dawn 'til dusk, she was never praised, but was often scolded for not being the best in her class. She didn't know that the real reason she couldn't be the best was that the subjects she studied were of no interest to her.

People said that Mirjam's childhood was a happy one. Her family had a nice house, money for finest foods and clothes, and she went to a prestigious school. But Mirjam often felt sad and lonely. Her parents always busy working, they never had time to listen to her stories about what happened at school, how children looked at her differently because she had more material things than they did.

She was shy and didn't have many friends and those who would visit her house only wanted to play with the newest toys and games her parents bought her. Mirjam wanted to have friends so she would allow her visitors to take home the toys that they liked, as she was afraid that they wouldn't want to play with her anymore if she didn't. But when her mother found out about giving the toys away, she was mad at her for days and put all the nice toys away in the attic. When Mirjam's friends saw that there was nothing interesting to play with, they stopped coming over and Mirjam was alone again, left with the belief that she had to give people things they wanted in order to be liked.

When she got older and started dating, she always ended up with guys asking her to do things for them, like write an essay or do the math quiz or finish a project. Even when she became an adult and moved in with her boyfriend Paul, she seemed to be doing all the housework and helping him with his work assignments, while he sat in front of television drinking beer. But she didn't mind, as he was there with her, saying he loved her and all that she did for him. She craved the moments of affection, like holding hands during a walk or soft kisses throughout the day for no reason at all. But she was content with the seldom intimate moments they shared at night.

Mirjam grew up to be an intelligent beautiful lady, but for some reason she always dressed in blacks and grays and didn't like to stand out from the crowd. She was hiding a soft inner center, a sensitive young lady who loved to paint, behind a cold façade of an accounting clerk. When she was alone, she allowed herself to dream of a different life, one where she would be an eccentric artist sharing life with a man who would understand her passions and treat her like a princess. But then there was a voice in her head that reminded her to come back to the earth and be grateful for having a steady job and a man who wanted to be with her. So she shut down her dream world and tried to forget about any possibility of another life.

Mirjam always read a lot and "new age" and "psychology" were her favorite bookstore sections. She was amazed by the stories of how people developed their inner confidence by practicing some self-improvement system or how they made their dreams happen as if by magic. She read books about women who changed from ugly ducklings into beautiful swans. She read about millionaires who started out as children of poor Eastern-European immigrants. She loved the story of a shepherd who left everything to go look for his treasure. Sometimes she thought that maybe she could be like him too. But then she remembered that she wasn't as strong or as smart or as brave... and so she would go back to dream in hiding from her own inner judge.

One day, she was sent to a training course by her boss. It was supposed to be a motivational workshop that people from different companies attended. That day, all that she ever read and thought impossible to apply proved to be possible for her. The trainer turned out to be a lovely older lady who explained to her (well, to the whole group, but to Mirjam it sounded like the words were spoken directly to her heart) that she had her inner power to make things happen, and showed her ways to bring this power forward.

Mirjam was surprised at herself, how believing in her own power became easier as she practiced being positive and changing her beliefs. She realized how abusive her relationship was, not just the one, but all of them from the past. Soon her boyfriend moved out and she felt a bit scared that she might end up alone forever. But she was willing to take a chance and start respecting herself instead of giving in to her insecurities. She connected the dots that lead from her present to her past and she made a first really conscious choice - not to let her past affect her future.

1.

WHAT IS LIFE?

"Life is a sum of all your choices."
~ Albert Camus ~

I will not fool myself or lie to you by pretending I know the only true answer to this. For centuries people have asked themselves the same question. Philosophers, poets, scientists and spiritual teachers, they all meditated on this - most important to humans subject.

"...that the cycles of life are endless - and always serve you, because life is a process that serves Life Itself."
~ Neale Donald Walsch ~

"I don't want to get to the end of my life and find that I just lived the length of it. I want to have lived the width of it as well."
~ Diane Ackerman ~

"He only lives, who living enjoys life."
~ Menander ~

"Carpe diem! Rejoice while you are alive; enjoy the day; live life to the fullest; make the most of what you have. It is later than you think."
~ Horace ~

We are here, on Earth, for a period of time (as far as we know it, putting faith aside), there must be some reason, a purpose to our existence. Without adding some sense, some meaning to Life, we feel lost, confused, depressed and may even lose the will to live altogether ...

"He who has a 'why' to live can bear almost any 'how'."
~ Friedrich Nietzsche ~

So we search for the answers and look for the meaning of this mysterious phenomenon that creates out days, months, and years and ultimately ends leaving those behind wondering about the afterlife, but that's a theme for another book.

I don't have one true answer to life's purpose. I am not omniscient and each of you will define life according to their own preferences, but I will tell you what I have learned life to be. And I'm pretty sure that whatever goals or dreams you may have, this explanation will sound as true to you as it does to me.

Life is an amazing journey.
It is an experience.
Life is to be lived and enjoyed.
And the purpose of Life is to be happy.
Your Life is yours and yours only and it is *you* who decides how to live it.
It's ALL up to you.
Your Life.
Your Journey.
Your experience.
Your happiness.

Now, what happiness means to you is a personal choice and that's when it becomes more interesting. The beauty of the world is not being, having, and doing the same things as our friends, family, or neighbors.

So your dad drives a Mercedes, but you always had a soft spot for the Beetle. That's completely fine. You have the right to choose what car you want to drive.

Your friends all wear skinny jeans, but you like the classic Levi's. That's great! Show your individuality!

Your family has always been in the medicine business, but you have artistic soul and want to sing. Do it! That is your life and you have a right to make it whatever you want.

We don't all want the same things and it's the diversity that makes life experiences interesting.

It takes courage to stand up for what you want and to make your own life choices. In our society, we have been led to believe that being different is something bad, that only if you follow the crowd you will be accepted and safe, that by fulfilling your parents' or partner's expectations you will be loved. That is an illusion, a lie that lets those "higher" on the society ladder control you. That is not what your soul longed for when it descended to this material plane. In order to really experience life, you need to have freedom to create a life of your own.

YOUR LIFE IS WHAT YOU BELIEVE

The interesting thing is that however people see life, it becomes true to them. We define the world, people, and ourselves through the lens of our beliefs and experiences. Each person creates their own private reality and the laws of their world can be completely different from those of other people's, or from what we call objective reality. But I want to emphasize that there are but a few actually objective truths in the world. One such thing might be gravity. But even gravity can be someday challenged, just as Copernicus challenged the belief that the world was flat.

So instead of being judgmental of other people's beliefs and opinions, we should all acknowledge that every human being has a right to live their own life and make their own choices. Instead of asking whether this person is right, or whether I am, one should concentrate on more important issue - whether the person's beliefs and choices work for their highest benefit and whether the person's actions do not hurt others in the process.

Imagine, for example, a woman who believes that her role in a relationship is to serve her husband. She will most likely be married to a man who believes that his wife should serve all his needs and wants. In her reality, that is how the world works, maybe because she learned that from her own mother or it derives from her own low self-esteem. Whatever the reason, she created the life that confirms her beliefs. And that would be fine. Except - is she happy and fulfilled in such relationship, as a human being? Is she experiencing the love and joy on her journey? If she is not happy, than something is wrong here. Her beliefs are taking away her ability to make life choices that are best for her.

On another hand, imagine that your son spends all his time playing soccer. But you are worried. You wanted him to become a lawyer, to have a stable, good income in the future, so you disapprove of his hobby. But is his choice really wrong? How can you know that? His passion is what makes him happy and it doesn't hurt anyone, maybe except your ego ... He too has a right to choose his life.

BELIEFS

I mentioned that your beliefs have a role in the process of creating your reality. I didn't mention though how huge of a role it is. Where do those beliefs come from and why are they so powerful?

"If you believe you can, you probably can. If you believe you won't, you most assuredly won't. Belief is the ignition switch that gets you off the launching pad."
~ Denis Waitley ~

When we come to this world, we're clean as a blank sheet of paper on which our history will be written. All we want is to love and experience this wonderful material reality. We learn about the world, life, and ourselves from the people closest to us - our parents, siblings, friends, and teachers. We are pure and innocent and we believe that people around us are just like us, that everything they tell us comes from their heart and is for our highest good. So we take it all as an undeniable truth. We believe it and take it as our own.

In the meantime, we experience many different situations, meet new people that treat us in different ways, sometimes even terrible things happen to us that we don't know how to deal with. We act and react, think, judge, imagine. And all that adds to our belief system.

Later, as we grow, those beliefs become so deeply rooted within our being that we don't even notice they exist. We take them as a part of our character, forgetting that we learned them at some point in life. Forgetting that those beliefs are just thoughts that we thought for a long time until we gave them power to control us. And forgetting that most of those beliefs are not even our own.

Not to blame our parents or teachers, they did the best they could in their own view. They taught us whatever they thought was necessary for our survival and happiness. Our parents are also a product of years of experiences and beliefs that took charge of their actions. Sometimes, they hurt us, put us down, or ignored us, but do you think they were aware of how these actions affected us? Probably not. Would anyone consciously harm another, especially someone as close to the heart as their own child, if they were aware? Sometimes, people are so caught up in their own world that every action, every word, every thought they have, however irrational, is justified in their own minds. So let's not blame the parents, but better see how we can be more aware of *our* behavior instead.

We live our lives *unaware*. And this is exactly where the power of our beliefs comes from - they lie hidden in our inner minds, disguised as part of us, driving us to behave in specific ways in particular situations, forcing us to make choices in life that are not always the best for us. In the whole process we are not even aware of the huge impact those hidden thoughts have on our existence.

~◎❀❀◎~

HABITS

Beliefs that are acted upon long enough become habits. Habits are even more disguised than the beliefs. They cling to you, pretending they are your "preferences," so you accept them as part of your lifestyle, not knowing how much they actually destroy your freedom, self-worth, and very often even your health. When you realize they are not acting in your favor, you're usually so used to them that giving them up seem impossible.

"Habit is a second nature which prevents us from knowing the first, of which it has neither the cruelties nor the enchantments."
~ Marcel Proust ~

Most commonly known habits - smoking, drinking, drugs - come from trying to make yourself feel better. There is a part of a person that believes he's not good enough or feels guilty or is afraid. These things cloud the reality for a short while, giving the illusion that the painful feeling disappeared. But then the feeling comes back, so he needs another fix and so on and so on. And when at some point he realizes what the feeling behind the habit was - the actual motivation and belief that pushed him into such destructive behavior - he might not be able to recover.

Let's look at some less obvious habits, as well. These might not be recognized as equally harmful as substance abuse, but they reinforce your negative beliefs nonetheless and can also destroy your happiness.

Do you feel like you always need to win at all costs in any situation?

You may be a perfectionist, needing to prove to yourself your own self-worth all the time. There is no such thing as "perfection" so you can drive yourself into exhaustion trying to reach it, while losing your friends and family because of your competitive attitude.

You just cannot stop yourself from making sarcastic comments and cutting remarks?

This is another example of self-confidence issue, creating a momentary illusion of you being better than someone, just to leave you feeling down and guilty soon afterwards. Although it may seem to you that you're being witty, such behavior is really hurtful to others and will result in making you very lonely.

Do you always say "yes" when people ask you for a favor, even if it doesn't suit you?

You may be thinking that doing things for others will make them like you and accept you more, but would a true friend appreciate only what you're doing for him or who you actually are? And where are *you* and your needs in such relations? There should always be balance of giving and receiving in all types of relationships.

Promising yourself to start exercising and always finding reasons not to do it?

You may be just lazy, but what if this is just a cover-up for the fear of failure? Or you might believe that you do not deserve to be fit and healthy. The only person that suffers as a result is you.

Do you fail to recognize your achievements, but always see your mistakes?

Putting yourself down is a sign of low self-esteem and can lead you to self-doubt, apathy, or even depression.

Does your inner dialogue always concentrate on the negative aspects of each situation?

Worrying and negative thinking is one of the most common and most destructive habits in the history of humanity. Negativity clouds every moment of happiness, takes away your personal power, and creates a life of fear and discontent.

During an argument, do you always speak out of anger, only to later regret your words?

Expressing your emotions is important, but if it is done without thoughtfulness and awareness of the reasons behind the emotions, it can ruin any relationship.

Is there always someone to blame for your misfortunes?

Avoiding responsibility for your own life may seem safer, but do you really want to give away the power for creating your own life?

Do you constantly avoid some situations out of fear?

Just think of all the opportunities and wonderful experiences you might be missing.

Can you see now how such negative habits deriving from negative beliefs can impact a person's life? Do you see yourself in any of these examples? I though you just might.

Now that you are aware of the hidden forces at work, that were running your life up to this point, do you want to take back control of your life? Life really *is* what you make it.

> *"As human beings we can reflect and make choices because we are capable of self-awareness. The greater our awareness, the greater our possibilities for freedom."*
> ~ Gerald Corey ~

ILLUSSIONS

Finally, I would like to point your attention toward the value of some life choices people make, in order for you to avoid getting lost in the illusions that many people believe, only to be left lost, unfulfilled, and purely unhappy at the end of their journey.

I'm afraid that the world that we live in became very confusing. People are led to believe that *having* is the key to happiness. And although I am, of course, aware that we all need food and shelter and that comfortable environment and some mod and cons are important to most people, we seem to go beyond our normal needs and wants and look to fill the inner emptiness with the outer shine. Don't get me wrong - I enjoy dressing up like any other gal and I cannot imagine my life without a car. But my car is there to serve a purpose - it takes me places I want or need to go. My clothes express my individuality. And I don't own things just to *own* them but only if they serve me in some way.

Money has been created for a reason - it is an easier way of exchanging energy than the ancient trade and barter system.

Money is the means to gain that what brings you happiness. Money is not the happiness in itself. By surrounding yourself with things that have no actual purpose for you, you create an illusion of happiness, an illusion of life. Acquiring things cannot be a purpose of life in itself, as you will find that no matter how much you own, it will not satisfy the inner need for fulfillment.

I have found that only a few simple things are necessary for happiness - someone to love, something to do, some way to express yourself, and something to smile about. Everything else comes from that. Just think about it.

"Just living is not enough. One must have sunshine, freedom, and a little flower."
~ Hans Christian Andersen ~

Miracle of Following Your Dreams

It was a beautiful Sunday morning when Mirjam received a call from a recruitment agency that disturbed her joyful mood. She recently received a diploma in Arts, graduating in the top of her class, and couldn't stop smiling at the thought of what lay ahead of her. Until the phone rang.

She always loved painting, but her parents wanted her to have a "real job," so she studied economics in college and then got a job as an accountant in some unknown clothing company. She worked there for three boring years, always coming home too tired to pick up a brush and paint anything. She started sulking more and more as the days went by and finally completely lost interest in anything that wasn't necessary for her survival. The doctors called it "depression," told her to stay off work for a month, and gave her prescription for some pills that were supposed to make her feel better.

She didn't take the pills, but went to bed and slept and slept and slept. A week went by when she finally got up and didn't feel tired. She made breakfast and decided to clean up a bit. She tidied up the kitchen, the living room, and the bathroom. She changed her bed sheets and went through her closet, taking out things that she hasn't worn in at least a year. It was quite a big pile! She reached for the boxes on the bottom of the closet, hoping to find some empty ones to put the clothes in. The first one she opened had her painting tools. Slowly, she took them out and the memories started floating back to her. Sitting in a park, drawing trees. Watching her sleeping dog; and placing that on paper. Relaxing at her first boyfriend's flat after a romantic evening, covering blank canvas with the image of his face in the candle light... The memories awakened something in her, this feeling of excitement that she hadn't felt in a long, long time. She took out some paper and paints, sat on her balcony, and started painting the view of the city. She got lost in the process and hadn't even realized that she started humming some silly song, smiling at nothing in particular. When she looked at her creation hours later, she was filled with so much joy and a kind of tender elation, any traces of her recent sadness and hopelessness simply vanished from her heart.

So she understood that no pills helped her keep such state of euphoria, but only a permanent change in her life could do the trick. She needed to paint to be able to be fulfilled. The job that she didn't like was slowly killing her from the inside, taking away not only the enjoyment from her existence, but also affecting her health. Now was the time to make a decision and it was a hard one.

Although Mirjam has been working on her confidence since attending the memorable workshop, she was only at the beginning of her journey of self-discovery. Her inner strength developed slowly, now still open to all kind of sabotaging attacks.

She heard a voice in her head telling her to go back to her job, that she would never be able to make money by being an artist, and that she wasn't good enough to become a recognized painter. That voice was loud and strong and she curled in herself at its sound. She imagined her dark future, as a dirty homeless hippie painter, sitting on a sidewalk begging for money for food. She shrugged in fear.

But then a small, calm, soft voice emerged from behind the other one. That voice reminded her of the joy she just felt when she was lost in the painting process. It told her that there is a special power, bigger than any of us, which supports those who follow their dreams. This power will not let her become poor and homeless as she follows her inner calling, because fulfilling that calling is the only way to be happy. The voice told her that it's everyone's divine right to use their gifts to create a happy life for themselves and spread that joy to everyone they meet on their journey.

Mirjam listened to the voices for a long time before making her decision. She knew she had a secure but unhappy life ahead of her if she went back to being an accountant. And there was no certainty if she left the job and followed her artistic dreams, but there was a chance for happiness. So despite her fears, she rang her boss and gave him two weeks' notice, then and there, before she'd have a chance to change her mind. Next day, she signed up at the Art College she always dreamed of attending.

She spent two wonderful years improving her painting skills and was now working on her portfolio, hoping to get a showcase with one of the art galleries in the city.

And then she got a call from recruitment agency. She left her accounting CV with them one day after a phone conversation with her mother, who reminded her how very unlikely it was to earn a living by being an artist. Now the recruitment agent rang and gave her a very promising job opening description at a big insurance company, a job with a great paycheck, health benefits, and room for promotion.

Mirjam was confused. She had her portfolio half ready and got a number from a friend of a friend to an open-hearted gallery owner that liked to promote new talents. But this accounting job would give her so much stability and financial security and maybe her mom would finally be proud of her …

She sat down at her balcony, hoping for an answer that would clear away the clouds that filled her heart. But only when she looked into her heart did she know that the only way to go on was to follow its call.

2.

WHAT DRIVES YOU?

I'd like to talk to you about your motivations. Without a motivation, you would not even get out of bed in the morning. Not to talk about reaching some higher goals. In order to do anything, you need to have an important reason to do it. The motivation. The drive.

> *"When you know what you want, and you want it badly enough, you'll find a way to get it."*
> ~ Jim Rohn ~

Various theories have been made throughout history about the driving forces of human behavior. Some say motivation comes from a basic need to minimize pain or maximize pleasure. Others get more specific, talking about satisfying the need for food and shelter or rest. Then there are deeper reasons, such as getting a desired job, helping others, making yourself feel better, or wanting to fulfill a duty. There is a theory, very popular in the psychological community, called Maslow's Hierarchy of Needs. It classifies basic survival needs that have to be obtained first so that one can then reach for the higher goals.

Maslow's Hierarchy of Needs Chart

That's definitely true and surely shows how different needs and motivations are in different social classes, cultures or countries. One will not think about their self-esteem when they lack food to put on the table.

Apart from survival needs, I have found that no matter what goal one wants to reach or need one has to satisfy, human motivation can come from two basic sources: from Love or from Fear.

LOVE

We are born to love. We come to this Earth filled with divine love for all creation. We love ourselves, we love people around us, we love the animals, the plants, the ground that we walk on, and the air that we breathe. We love life.

This is the natural state of our soul. Any action that comes from the place of Love will not harm any living creature. It will not harm us. By being in the state of *unconditional love*, we are able to experience the world in its magnificence. We are able to see the divinity in everything that happens in our lives. We're able to see it from the higher perspective of being the spark of God experiencing the material world.

"I will reveal to you a love potion, without medicine, without herbs, without any witch's magic; if you want to be loved, then love."
~ Hecaton of Rhodes ~

For some reason, many people lose the ability to think, speak, and act from the place of Love in the course of their lives. They crumble under the pressure of others, lost and unhappy themselves. They learn to judge people and situations based on their own fears and beliefs. They become scared, hurt, and at times angry and spiteful. They forget about the Love they always have inside them.

A person driven by Love can be spotted from a far away. That's the boy helping an old lady to cross the street. That's the girl helping at the animal shelter on the weekends. That's the nurse that will stay longer with a patient, just to hold his hand until he falls asleep. That's a mother supporting her son accused in court of robbery.

A loving person speaks to others kindly and acts with kindness, is understanding and tolerant. Also positive, as Love shows that all is well no matter what happens. That is the person who chooses whatever is best for him in his life, knowing that by loving himself and loving others he cannot go wrong.

Making choices from the place of Love means taking care of yourself and others, concentrating on inner growth instead of outer possessions. It is living in awareness of one's actions and their consequences, understanding the importance of experiencing life fully and being happy as our sole purpose and duty in the world.

⊷⊰⊱⊶

FEAR

Hate is not the opposite of Love. Fear is. Hate is a by-product of Fear, the same as anger, judgment, sadness, selfishness, embarrassment, defensiveness, bitterness, guilt, and shame. All these feelings and more are disguises of Fear. They are coping mechanisms the person learned in order not to feel afraid, for Fear can be strong, powerful, and even paralyzing.

"Fear is pain arising from the anticipation of evil."
~ Aristotle ~

While Love gives power to the person, Fear takes it away. And what do we do when we feel powerless over our own lives? We look for ways to get that power back by any means necessary. Often, just getting the illusion of the power satisfies us temporarily, like in a case of anger. You scream at your child, feeling a momentary power over him, but you don't get back the power over yourself. Or you become critical of others, making mean remarks, deluding yourself that you are better than them. Or maybe you act selfishly, putting yourself first, no matter how many people that hurts, for the fear of not getting what you think you need.

People acting out of Fear create chaos and sadness around them. They hurt themselves and others. They make hectic choices and often regret them later. Letting Fear drive you is very destructive to your life and the lives of those around you. Look at Hitler. He was so afraid of not being good enough, that he created mad quest for power that killed millions of people.

Fighting Fear with anything but Love will never create happiness. Remember, though, that Fear is learned, so it can be un-learned. Love is a natural state of being.

"Fears are nothing more than a state of mind"
~ Napoleon Hill ~

FEAR OF LOSS OF LOVE

What is the one thing that each person, no matter what gender, culture, religion, age or social class wants? What one thing can make one climb to the highest mountains of their abilities? Or if unfulfilled, can make a person drown in the sea of despair? It's the need to be loved and accepted the way we are. Everyone needs that. No exceptions. You may say that you don't care what people think about you, whether they accept you or not, but deep inside, you crave for even one person to say: *"Hey, I like you just because you exist."* That makes you feel good. You may say you don't need anyone to love you, but you would only be playing a pretend game, lying to yourself not to feel the pain of being lonely.

We, humans - people are social beings. We were not created to be alone. It is through interactions with other people and our environment that we get to experience life and learn about ourselves. Sure, some of us prefer to spend time alone, maybe reading or listening to music. Some like bigger groups of people while others prefer to have just a couple of close friends. Some people believe in marriage and a huge family, others are happy with only their friends. That's fine. Each one of us is different. But spending time alone at times doesn't mean you want to be alone all the time, always and forever. All of your life. It would be a sad and uninteresting life without other people. Even Tarzan, living in a jungle without people, joined a family of animals.

It's natural and completely fine to want to be with others, to be loved and accepted. That's a basic human need. And to have that need met, people go to great distances, sacrificing their time, money, dignity, even life. For the fear of losing the love and affection is the biggest fear of all.

It starts in childhood when we learn that we need to be "good" to get our parents' affection, and if we're not behaving as expected, then we're called "bad" and the affection is withdrawn or we get punished. The child learns that love needs to be earned, that he needs to be someone the parents want him to be to be accepted, that it's not ok just to be himself. Children are so pure an innocent, they know that they came here to give love unconditionally and then we teach them that the love is conditional, that acceptance is gained by specific behavior, fitting in with societal norms or family expectations. That's very sad, as this process we call "raising" is actually destroying a person's individuality and freedom to be.

If your parents were loving and accepted you unconditionally, you are very lucky. But still you probably had to fit in with other norms when attending school, getting first jobs, and starting relationships. A child with good self-esteem will surely have it easier in adulthood, as he would understand that he doesn't have to change to gain love and acceptance. But most children have not been brought up in supporting environments and as adults enter destructive relationships, take abusing jobs and suffer a great deal of pain and sorrow.

To avoid that and to free yourself from the fear of not being loved and accepted, you need to understand and believe one thing: you are unique - there is no other person just like you in the whole world. You are amazing and lovable just because you exist. You are special and you don't need to earn that.

I will tell you a secret you probably already know, but just forgot to remember. If you love and accept yourself, others will accept and love you, as well. When love shines out from your heart towards yourself, you will meet only such people on your path that are loving, kind, and accepting. So in order to have love and acceptance in your life, you only need to change your feelings towards yourself.

Love yourself.
Accept yourself.
You are beautiful.

☙❦❧

FEAR OF THE UNKNOWN

If you are like most people, you are a creature of habit. You have your little daily rituals, you do some things in special ways, you like your coffee with the same amount of sugar and milk each time. Those little habits give you a feeling of control over your environment. If you are like most people, you like to know what happens tomorrow, you plan some things in advance, you check the map before you go places, or at least take a map with you. To be able to predict how your life happens also gives a sense of control. If you are like most people, you might go on holidays to places you don't know, but in your daily life you stick to what is familiar to you. Familiarity lets you feel in control.

People like to be able to control their lives for one simple reason - control gives a sense of safety and security. And it is a basic human instinct to be safe.

I support the need for safety with all my heart. I don't agree with reckless behavior and putting yourself in danger's way. I lock my door when I leave my house and I don't walk at night in dark alleys. Life is the most precious gift and one needs to protect it within his means and reason.

The problem arises when a person tries to excessively control his environment. As I said - we need to be protective of our life within reason. You cannot avoid every danger possible, as you don't have an ability to predict the future. Such avoidance will prevent you from enjoying and experiencing your life.

That is a very common mistake - trying to control your environment. Some even stretch it out to trying to control other people and their behavior. You cannot control the world or others. The only thing you can control is yourself. You can control your thoughts, your feelings and your actions. You can *choose* your thoughts, your feelings and your actions. And by controlling and making choices within yourself, you can make changes in your life that will create *real* safety and security: the security within. The safety of knowing that you can depend on yourself, that by making the right choices for you, you can protect your life, and create it in any way you like.

If you're wondering about changing other people, you should know that by changing yourself, others will change how they behave around you ... But we'll go back to that in another chapter.

Why do people like to be in control? Because they fear the unknown.

People tend to stick to what is familiar to maintain that comfortable feeling of being in control of their life, that illusion of control over one's environment. That creates a very common problem - being afraid of change. Did you ever hear the expression *"better known hell than unknown heaven?"*

I used to wonder why so many women live in abusive relationships. They are usually smart, pretty, capable women. But they stay in relationships with men who continuously hurt them. Do they not see that they can just get up and leave? Yes, no matter what excuses they tell themselves why they can't do it, it is that simple. Make a choice to leave. Start respecting yourself and create a different life. The first real reason for not leaving I found is low self-esteem. They do not believe that they can make it on their own. So sad that they cannot see how much strength it takes them to live such a life! But another reason is the fear of change: *"How is my life going to be? What will happen? Will I manage? At least in this life I know what awaits me every day."* The fear of the unknown takes away their power and in result destroys their lives.

Are you afraid of the unknown? Do you ever take chances? Do you make choices in life that will take you places you've never been?

I will tell you one more secret - the only constant thing in life is *change*. Just as nature changes with each season, our lives continuously change. We can be the forerunner of those changes or we can let life take us where it wants us to go. If we fight the change, we will lose. Therefore, I encourage you to create the change. That is the only way you can have some control over your unknown. No one can predict the future, but by making choices to create changes that you want, you allow the natural flow of Universe into your life. That is your best shot at knowing how your life will turn out.

> *"To exist is to change, to change is to mature, to mature is to go on creating oneself endlessly."*
> ~Henri Bergson ~

Befriend the Unknown. If you look at the times in your past when you took a leap of faith and stepped onto foreign grounds,

I'm sure you will see that those unfamiliar roads took you to the places that enriched your life. Experiences on these unknown paths made you who you are today. And you are wonderful, aren't you?

❧❀❧

FEAR OF DEATH

Very close to the Fear of the Unknown is the Fear of Death. We don't know what happens when we die, do we? Some people have had clinical death experiences, so they have a vague idea. But most of us need to go on faith.

What do you believe about the afterlife?

I personally believe in reincarnation. I like to have "proofs" of the things I believe in and I did have some past life experiences in sessions of hypnotic regression, therefore my faith has some ground to be built on. But even before these explorations, I was curious about life and death. I read about different faiths, various beliefs, and I chose those beliefs that suited me, the kind of beliefs about death that supported me in life. These are the only beliefs worth having.

So think about your faith and what it tells you about death? Does it make you feel reassured? Does it bring you peace of mind and heart? If not, you might want to do some searching in order to find beliefs that work for your benefit.

From what I've learned and what I've said a few times already, we come to the Earth to experience. We come from somewhere. And I'm not talking about our physical bodies. Bodies are part of the material world. What makes our bodies work? What is that part that thinks, feels, and experiences? That is the Soul. That is the part that came into the material world and when it is done experiencing, it will return to where it came from, with new knowledge and understanding. After some time, it may chose to come back here again, to experience something else. Or if it has fulfilled its search, it may want to stay with the Source. Or in Heaven, as some call it.

If that is what I believe, I have nothing to fear about death. It's just a transformation into another realm, into a place of unconditional Love. Why wouldn't I want to go there?

Well, some people believe in Hell and Purgatory. But do you really think that the One who created you, the One that your soul is a part of, the "Father Above" would do so just to punish you for what you've experienced? The whole purpose of living is the experiences. And in the divine realm of Love, there is no such concept as "right" or "wrong." There are just experiences and they are not to be judged, they are only to be learned from.

The concept of Hell has been created by people in power, in order to create a fear of punishment in others. If people accepted their self-proclaimed laws and behaved in ways their "masters" wanted them to, they were easier to control. As a result, the people in power could keep on living under an illusion that they were better than others and pretended that they had no fears themselves.

What if you don't believe in God or reincarnation or Heaven or anything at all? Do you really? Just think about the world and imagine how it could have been created in such a magnificence of detail. Is it even possible that it was just a chance?

Remember, your beliefs should support you, not work against you. Choose your faith wisely and you will conquer the fear of death.

"We're not wanting to be insensitive to what so many of you are feeling, but we are very much wanting you to put this death thing in the proper perspective: You are all going to die! Except there is no death. You're all going to make your transition into Non-Physical. It is time to stop making your transition into Non-Physical sound like a subject that is uncomfortable and begin acknowledging that it is something that happens to everyone. This death thing is so misunderstood that you use it to torture yourself never-endingly and just absolutely unnecessarily. There are those who feel such fulfillment of life and such Connection to Source Energy, who understand that there is no separation between what is physical and Non-Physical; who understand that there is not even a lapse in consciousness, that "death" is a matter of closing one's eyes in this dimension and literally opening one's eyes in the other dimension. And that, truly, is how all death is, no matter how it looks, up to that point... The re-emergence into Source Energy is always a delightful thing."

~ Abraham ~

❧

FEAR OF FAILURE

In our world, competitiveness became very important. People want to win, to get ahead. To reach something, to gain something, to achieve. By setting your life within this frame of mind, you will easily become the victim of the fear of failure.

For most of us, it's our parents that taught us that achievements and winning are important. That is what their parents taught them. All nations are built upon people wanting to get higher on the society level. We're told that being famous, rich, or successful means that we're better people.

Do you believe that?

I don't. I believe that success means being a good person, being loving and kind to yourself and others. Being happy and living your life consciously. If you reach for things outside of yourself to make you feel better, you will surely be disappointed, for only if you're working on your inner beauty you will be able to create the beauty in your outer experience.

Just look around you. Read the papers, tabloids even. So many rich and successful people are not happy. They become drug or alcohol addicts, they get depressed, they cannot stay in a relationship. Is that really a successful life? Or is it just an illusion?

Now what is failure? If you reach for something and don't get it, you usually will call it a failure. Some people are so set on reaching those things they consider important that the fear of failure becomes their strongest driving force. Although some may think it's a positive motivation, I cannot agree.

What happens if you don't get that position you applied for? Of you don't win that first place in the marathon? You beat yourself up. You feel bad about yourself. You put yourself down. You lose your self-esteem and you become unhappy.

That is not supportive at all. That does not benefit your life. On the other hand, if you had a desire to fulfill your goal along with understanding that it's the journey that matters most, not the destination, that would surely change your feelings about not winning, wouldn't it?

I don't believe in failure. To me such a thing doesn't exist. Every experience is a lesson to be learned from. If something didn't come out the way you planned, that is only for you to learn how to do it better the next time. Or maybe this situation had a deeper lesson for you, a lesson about your own self or the meaning of life? Or maybe it was to show you that you're on the wrong path and should re-examine your life?

"Don't be afraid to fail. Don't waste energy trying to cover up failure. Learn from your failures and go on to the next challenge. It's OK to fail. If you're not failing, you're not growing."
~Anne Sullivan ~

There are no failures, just lessons.

OTHER FEARS

There are many more fears that make a huge impact on the way people choose to live their life, such as fear of embarrassment, or fear of rejection, or criticism, or maybe old age or poverty. Even fear of heights can be strong enough to limit a person's experience. To me, they all come from the above mentioned main fears. The point is - if you realize that these fears exist in your psyche, would you choose to let them run your life? Or would you take the control into your own hands and say - no more!

So take a minute now to think - what drives you?
Love or Fear? ...

"The key to change is to let go of fear."
~ Roseanne Cash ~

Miracle of Self-Worth

Mirjam's mother often called her oversensitive. When she was small, Mirjam brought home stray cats, injured birds, or other little creatures. She remembers trying to resuscitate a fly once, to no avail, of course, but she cried for days after that bug was gone. She would always try to help out her less fortunate friends, giving them her school lunch or her new pencils. When she watched "Lassie Come Home" and "Bambi", she felt such sadness and then anger at the "mean" people that she wouldn't speak to anyone for two weeks.

Her mother scolded her for being such a cry-baby, so with time, Mirjam started to feel ashamed of her feelings and made sure not to show them in public. But she kept suffering still, her emotions so strong that often they wouldn't let her sleep at night. It wasn't just the news about people treating each other or the animals badly that affected her deeply, the worst was when mean words or actions were directed at her. Whenever someone commented on her in a slightly negative way, she thought about it for days, she cried into her pillow for hours at a time and felt as if nobody liked her. She often said that people make her feel sad. So she did all she could to conform to the standards set by people around her, thinking that if she was just like them, they would accept her and the sadness would go away. Sometimes it worked, but often she had to give much more from herself. She always loved to help people and was a good listener, so she didn't mind helping friends and co-workers with whatever they asked of her. She would feel happy when she was needed and only sometimes, when she had a problem she wanted to talk about and her friends seemed to be too busy, she felt a sharp needle stabbing her heart... But she brushed off such moments as fast as she could. She couldn't afford to let her emotions ruin things again.

Mirjam changed not only her looks to fit the others, but with time she also started acting like them. People had tough lives where she lived, so complaining was the way they carried their conversations. They complained about low wages and high prices. They nagged about the government and health care system. They were jealous about those who had more than they did and whined that their fate was unjust. Their husbands were always lazy bastards and their wives were mean hags. Their children were lazy and stupid and their bosses were exploiting them. They always had pains and aches that uneducated doctors couldn't fix, and the weather was either too hot or too cold. Mirjam learned to speak that way really easily, her mother already taught her to look at herself in negative way long time ago. To speak ill of everything else was just a small step.

As she got really good at complaining, her world started to change. Her boss started to be more demanding to her and often scolded her for no reason. She met people who spoke nicely to her face, but mean behind her back. Her car broke down often and she started getting colds and sniffles every couple of months. Whenever things like that happened to her friends, they would go out for drinks to make themselves feel better. She went with them once and actually forgot about all the problems for a couple of hours. She woke up with terrible headache the next day and promised herself she would never do it again. But as she kept on complaining, bad things kept on happening to her, so she kept on drowning her sorrows with the evening drinks. She blamed bad luck for her unhappy existence.

One night, coming home after another party, Mirjam saw a homeless man sitting on the street holding a piece of cardboard with a few words written on it:

NO ONE CAN MAKE YOU FEEL INFERIOR
WITHOUT YOUR CONSENT

She wondered: "Do I let people make me feel inferior? Unworthy? Small?"

She knew that she did. She knew very well that she craved other's acceptance more than anything else. She also knew that this need was destroying who she really was. There was another person deep inside her who didn't like who Mirjam became - the little sensitive girl, who preferred painting pictures to going to wild parties, a person who once saw only good in others and the world, someone who had potential to be happy if she only didn't care what others thought so much ... Could she become such person again if she really wanted to?

3.

WHAT IS CHOICE?

According to the Bible, when God created Adam and Eve in Paradise, he gave them the ability to choose. He didn't just create thoughtless robots that automatically loved him and surrendered to all his wishes. He gave them *Free Will*. They could obey him or not. He put the Tree of Knowledge in Paradise, so people could choose whether to eat its fruits and learn of the "good and evil" or whether to obey the law and live in oblivion. It was intentional.

In a grand scale of the divine design, we are born to experience Life. In non-material, spiritual state we can only experience Love. But in order to really appreciate that Divine Love, God's spark within us wanted to experience contrast and diversity. It is only through that contrast, through experiencing ups and downs, highs and lows, beauty and ugliness, love and fear, that we can really see what the Divine Love actually is.

If you've never seen the rain, do you know what a sunny day looks like?

If you've never been sick, do you know how important health is?

If you've never feared, do you recognize love?

We come to this material reality as a part of the Source to experience all aspects of the world and to find our way back to Unconditional Love through the power of Free Will. Furthermore, we start making choices even before we come into this reality. Being in a pure soul state, we reflect on the experiences we've had in previous lifetimes and decide what it is that we want to experience this time. It's hard to understand sometimes if we decide to be born as poor or sick. But it's important to remember that it is by overcoming those hard circumstances and by learning the lessons they carry that we can liberate ourselves from their burden and move on towards the next chapter of our current lives and towards Love.

"It is not good for all your wishes to be fulfilled: through sickness you recognize the value of health, through evil the value of good, through hunger satisfaction, through exertion, the value of rest."
~ Heraclitus ~

A big part of this earthly learning experience is becoming aware that it is not our outside circumstances that create our happiness or unhappiness, it is only our internal attitude towards those circumstances. The biggest choice that we have in life is HOW WE FEEL.

You may be broke, alone, and sick, but still you can be happy at the sight of a butterfly dancing between flowers on a sunny day. Actually, we can see from many biographies that it's the people who had a though life, who experienced pain and suffering, who were often happier that those who had it easy. You not only learn what is really important in life by experiencing troubles, but you also find out how powerful you actually are! By choosing to be positive, to feel love and joy, you realize that those feelings are a starting point to create a better, happier, and more fulfilling life.

"A pleasant and happy life does not come from external things: man draws from within himself, as from a spring, pleasure and joy."
~ Plutarch ~

There is a great movie by Roberto Benigni *Life is Beautiful,* that shows a story of a Jewish man named Guido who was put into the concentration camp with his son during World War II. In this camp, Nazis separated adults from children, so he hid his son in order to save his life and to spare him the terrible pain of this situation. He pretended the whole thing was just a game, and the person who got 1000 points would win a tank. Guido chose to make the situation work for him and his son, he chose to act positively no matter what. He chose to keep the faith that one day his son would be rescued and would survive.

Guido made his choices facing what seemed to be a hopeless situation. He made the choice to act and to feel certain way - to be positive no matter what. Don't you think that you can make your choices, too?

Remember, you cannot change the outside world, nor you can change other people by forcing change upon them. But you can change the way you feel about the world or other people. You can choose to take things personally, to cry and wallow in despair, to give up hope, and to cover your fear and pain with illusions of money, power, or fame. Or you can choose to see the divine lesson in each situation, to appreciate everything that is happening as a choice you made a long time ago (or before you were born) and to be positive and grateful for each moment that you live. Whether you choose the first or the second option will determine the quality and depth of your existence and it will also affect how your future life will be.

CHOSING THE FEELINGS

"Our ultimate freedom is the right and power to decide how anybody or anything outside ourselves will affect us."
~ Stephen Covey ~

You must realize that there is nobody or nothing that can make you feel, think, or act in a certain way. You are the only one who has access to your mind and your emotions. There is no outside force stronger that your own inner power. You choose how you feel. You choose how you act based on those feelings. You choose what to think about a person or a situation.

So often, people say: *"HE made me angry."* Is it really that person that made you so angry? Did he plug you into the outlet that says "Anger" and pushed ON button? Of course, there is no such outlet. But he unconsciously did push the button, though, but not the "Anger" one. His behavior or words touched something in you that was painful and that is why you felt the way you did. So instead of blaming the other person and talking about what he did to make you angry, look within and ask yourself: *"What am I really angry about? What is that thing in me that hurts so much that I react with anger? Which of my fears were awakened by his words?"*

Once you realize the real reason for your feelings, you can actually start working on releasing those painful or scary thoughts from your mind. You will not react the same way to that person's words again. Your relationship will improve and you will get your power back - the power to choose your feelings, not to react to hidden thoughts of beliefs in your subconsciousness.

Your feelings are indicators of your inner state of being. You have positive beliefs about yourself and the world, which serve you well and bring happiness and fulfillment into your life. And you have negative beliefs about yourself and the world, such that restrict you from reaching your full potential. Your feelings show you whether you are in a positive or negative state of being, or in other words - are you allowing or disallowing the goodness into your life? Your feelings are your guidance system. They are an important tool for you to see what is going on inside of your mind.

If you learn to become aware of your feelings in different situations and then examine them, you will learn about your subconscious thoughts, beliefs, and habits. From then, you can work on changing those thoughts, beliefs, and habits. Once you change your thoughts, your life will take a turn towards whatever it is that you dream of.

Your feelings are also your driving force. You can create your life as you want to, but you cannot do so while being overwhelmed by negative feelings. Once you become aware of the real reasons behind your sadness, guilt, or anger, you can choose to feel joy or gratitude instead. You can even make the choice now - before you even start examining those unpleasant emotions, that whenever they arise, you will only use them as an indicator of something deeper within you and immediately shift toward a feeling that serves you better. Why not? Why be a victim of your own emotional state? You can choose your emotional state! You *can* choose how you feel.

I am not telling you to deny your negative emotions. Pushing them away only makes them become as a volcano covered by a rock - at one point they will explode and create havoc in your life. If you feel something, it must be important. Do not deny the feeling. Realize that there is a reason behind it. Allow yourself to feel that emotion for a short while, but do not let it control you. Do not allow this emotion to run your life. Examine it. Understand it. Then - change it. The only thing that you can control in the whole wide world is yourself ...

CHOOSING THE THOUGHTS

"I think therefore I am."
~Rene Descartes ~

Common understanding of this sentence is that the action of "thinking" was a proof of one's existence. I think Descartes meant a great deal more than that ...

Let me shed a bit of light of the Law of Attraction onto these words: whatever you think of, you manifest into your existence. If you were not thinking of something, it would not exist.

Thoughts are very powerful. They are not mere ether that runs through your head and then disappears. Thoughts are energy just as anything else in the world. They vibrate on a specific level and they attract towards themselves that which is alike, in other words - whatever vibrates on the same level. (More thorough explanation of the Law of Attraction can be found in Chapter 8).

You think of having a baby, all of the sudden you see babies everywhere you look. You keep thinking of your friend from college and he calls you the next day. You are really worried about scratching your new car and someone backs into it in a parking lot.

Did anything like that ever happen to you? Of course, it did.

Thoughts create things. They attract into your life whatever it is that you keep thinking of. Whatever you think of for a while manifests into your life. In this simple way, your thoughts create your life!

Isn't it a wonderful to realize that you have such an enormous power over your own life? You can create things, make them happen, become whoever you want to be. Amazing!

So why are so many people creating things they don't want? See, you think *all the time*. You don't get a break from thinking. Most of us just let the thoughts run through our heads with no special plan. People don't choose what they think about. Their thoughts come from their inner beliefs or habits. Most of us are used to complaining and worrying about things. Now if you worry about losing your job, if you think that you don't want to lose your job, what are you constantly thinking about? Yes - losing your job! So without meaning to, you actually attract the situation you didn't want to happen into your life ... Whatever you think about, you manifest into reality.

There is no outside force that makes you think. You may notice things around you, but you don't have to concentrate your thoughts on them. Thinking something once doesn't give it a power to exist. But if you constantly think one thought over and over, you give it power. It becomes stronger and bigger to the point that it not only occupies all your mind, not letting other thoughts come to the surface, but it becomes so strong that is *materializes*.

So if that's how the thoughts work - don't you want to choose what you're thinking about? You can give into the habit of worrying about unwanted things happening or you can turn it around and actually think the opposite - think of what you *want* to happen.

Just imagine that you feel lonely. You would like to be in relationship. You want to have a companion. Your usual thoughts would be: *"I'm so lonely, nobody loves me. Men don't notice me. I will always be alone..."* And guess what? When you go out (if you actually get yourself to go out in such a state of mind) you send the signals to all the male population: *"I'm not likable. Don't notice me. Leave me alone."* And they don't notice you. You don't meet anyone. You stay alone.

If you took another route and changed your thought around to something like: *"I'm attractive. I'm ready to meet someone great. I can't wait to be in relationship."* you will see that wherever you go, men look at you, they smile at you, and soon enough you will meet many of them - and surely that special one!

Now imagine that you want to lose some pounds. You keep thinking: *"I'm so fat. I don't want to be fat. I have to stop eating sweets and fast food..."* and all you see around you are those tasty burgers and cakes and chips. You force yourself not to eat them, you may last a couple of days in complete agony, but finally you just cannot stop yourself from digging into them. And, probably, you will eat more that you're used to at this point, just because you created such an appetite for those foods! Pretty soon you will be as fat as you imagined yourself to be.

On the other hand, you may choose another thought:*"I want to be slim. I accept my beautiful body. I like to eat healthy foods. Vegetables are good and tasty."* And you actually start craving healthy foods, you see yourself slim in your mind, and sooner that you know - you will look just like you wanted!

Another example - imagine that you want to win the marathon. You train every day and keep thinking: *"Oh my god, there are so many miles to go, I don't think I can do it. This is sooo hard."* And while you train, you keep seeing others running faster than you, the road seems to stretch into hundreds of miles instead of five that it actually is, and your body becomes heavy and tired. When the time for the marathon comes, you will probably not even try to win it, you'll just run at slow pace and then feel bad for not trying harder.

Now if at the start of your training you choose to think: *"I am a great runner. I am fast, I am strong, I am a winner!"* the training will become easier and easier for you each day. On the day of the marathon, you will run with a smile on your face, all the time seeing yourself first at the finish line and surely enough - getting there first at the end.

This is the power of your thoughts. Choose them wisely. Choose them positively. Create your reality.

What if you're so used to the negative thoughts that you cannot even imagine that you can think differently? You need to start slowly by practicing your awareness. Be aware of your thoughts. Notice what you're thinking about. Use your emotional guidance system to pick the thoughts that don't serve you well. Then ask yourself: *"Is this thought true? Or is it just something I'm just used to thinking?"*

I like to have proof of whatever I'm doing, so in the process of choosing my thoughts I ask the next question: *"What are the proofs that this thought is true? What are the proofs that it is not true?"*

It is a learning process and it takes time. Start with awareness and follow it thorough with questioning. Then choose the thought that serves you better, the one that creates the life of your dreams.

"It is important to understand that counterproductive actions of body, speech and mind do not arise of their own accord, but spring up in dependence on our motivation. Faulty states of mind give rise to faulty actions. To control negative physical and verbal actions, we need to tame our minds."
~ Dalai Lama ~

CHOOSING THE WORDS

Words are the thoughts that you put out into the world. Voiced thoughts are like arrows sent out into the Universe. They have added speed and power. Also, it works in the opposite way - words add power to your thoughts. If you repeated a phrase often, it will surely be part of your life by now.

Ask yourself now: *"What words do I put out into the world?"*

"My job is hard."
"I am so tired."
"I've had a tough day."

"I have bad luck."
"I always get into trouble/lose my keys/get the worst seat."
"I never get a break/get anywhere/get what I want."
"Life sucks."

Just using the words "always" and "never" sets you up for life! If you ALWAYS end up in bad relationships, how can the next one be any better? If you NEVER get what you want, how can the Universe give it to you? *Always* means forever. *Never* does not let things happen.

Other words that are to be used with caution are "have to" and "should". They take away your power to choose. Honestly, you don't *have to* do anything. You can if you want to. You may feel you need to do it, but in the end, it is your choice if you do it or not. And who says you *should* do something? You do. You are the only one imposing rules on yourself. So why not use the word "want" instead? You *want* to do it. You have a choice whether to do it or not. Take back your right to choose!

Become aware of what you say to people. If someone asks you about your day, do you start by talking about all the bad stuff that happened or the good ones? Do you tend to complain or do you look for solutions for problems? Just notice what you talk about. Do these words support you in positive thinking or do they sabotage it?

Another thing - do you speak out of emotions, or do you let yourself think what you're going to say first? Words can hurt not only you, but others too. If you let the emotions overpower you, the words that come out are not always true. And you will regret them in pretty soon.

I always use this Spanish proverb when talking: *"Speak only when your words will improve the silence."*

༄☙❦☙❧

CHOOSING THE ACTIONS

The choice begins with the feeling and ends with the action. You may have chosen to pay attention to your emotions, think positive thoughts, and speak well to support them. To finish what you have started, you must seal your choice with the action. Nothing will happen out of its own accord. Nobody will do the work for you. If you chose which direction you want to proceed, you need to take the first step. Proceed, do, act.

Your actions should affirm your choices. You are making a statement to the world with your actions. You're saying loud and clear: *"This is me. This is what I believe. This is what I want. This is what I am doing to make me happy."*

Do you know how people say: *"I wish I won a million dollars in the lottery!"* But they haven't bought the ticket! How in the world they can get what they want if they don't even make the small effort of going to the store and getting the lottery ticket?

Yes, you start by choosing your thoughts, adding good feelings and speaking your truth. It sets your dreams in motion. The Universe starts working towards giving you the opportunities that will take you closer to what you want. But you must *be* in the world in order to be reached by those opportunities!

You don't have to have it all figured out right away - each step of your journey will be uncovered at the right time. You will make more choices on the way. But *do* step on the path! This is the last part of your choosing process - taking the first step and setting the wheels of the Universe in motion. You may choose not to do anything, to just stay where you are. Safely live the life you're accustomed to. Or you may chose to take a leap of faith and step into the Unknown, believing that by having the right thoughts and the right feelings you will flow towards ultimate happiness. Your own happiness, created by your choices.

You don't need to know the whole road to reach your destination. You just need to keep in mind what it is that you want and take that first step. Then keep your eyes open for the signs. Paulo Coelho writes beautifully about the signs in his *Alchemist*:

"In order to arrive you must follow the signs. God inscribed on the world the path that each man must follow. It is just a matter of reading the inscription he wrote for you."

Once you set sails toward what you want, once you make your choices and stick by them, the Universe responds to you by offering you opportunities. Signs are the language of the Universe that shows these opportunities. If you walk on your path with your eyes open, not only you will be amazed by the beauty of the world that you pass, you will see that nothing happens by accident. There is not one person that you meet without a reason. Everything around you conspires to help you to reach your dreams. You can keep your eyes open for the signs of opportunities and grab them as you go along. Or you may have to take a longer route and make more choices before you get there. But if you keep going true to your decision to reach your own private happiness, you will finally reach it.

Please be aware that your actions confirm your choices. Make sure that you allow the goodness to come to you. If you want to be in fulfilling relationship, do not go out on dates with the same type of person you used to date before. Do not choose the needy guy or the shallow guy or the show-off guy. Confirm you choice with the right action. Tell the world that you will go on dates, but only with the kind of person that can make you happy. If you want to be an internal decorator, send out your CV to the companies that deal with internal decoration, not to the department store near you. If you want to have loads of money, do not always buy the cheapest thing available. Buy the better shampoo sometimes. Show the Universe what you are expecting so that the Universe can respond back by sending the right opportunities your way.

What if you don't see any opportunities in front of you? What if you feel so stuck in the situation that you just cannot see a way out? Believe me - there is *always* a way out! You may have to check your thoughts again, re-examine your feelings, and find the beliefs that cloud your vision of your reality. Then keep your eyes open for the smallest, tiniest step that you can take just to get the ball rolling. Maybe you can just go for a walk, instead of staying in the house crying. Maybe you can get a haircut or buy a new dress. Or maybe decide to buy your morning coffee somewhere else from now on. Just do a small action with the belief that it will jump start the engine of your future!

"Your present circumstances don't determine where you can go; they merely determine where you start."
~ Nido Qubein ~

CHOOSING WISELY

Remember that just as you have free will, so do other people. You make your choices and you need to allow others to make theirs. Since we all are different, the happiness can mean opposite things to us.

So if you are looking for love, do not insist on being in the relationship with this particular man or woman. This person may not be the right person for you! Instead, concentrate on the qualities of the person you would like to be with. Think of how you want your future life to be. Allow the perfect person for *you* to come into your life.

If you want to get a job in the marketing department, do not say which company you want to work for. Just think of what you want to do at this job, what kind of people you want to work with, and what kind of atmosphere you want there to be. The universe will bring the right job to you!

Do not limit your opportunities by being too specific. Choose the overall qualities that you're looking for and be open to what comes your way!

"When someone makes a decision, he is really diving into a strong current that will carry him to places he had never dreamed of when he first made the decision."
~ Paulo Coelho ~

The Miracle of Following the Thread to the End

Mirjam remembers feeling scared a lot when she was younger. Adults around her told her stories that the children who didn't do what their parents told them to were taken away by the Bad Old Witch. Mirjam dreamed about the Witch often, always trying to scream at the top of her lungs, but no voice came out. She'd wake up right before the old hag grabbed her ... Mirjam made sure to do everything adults asked of her, just so the Witch would stay away. With time, she got into habit of not asking "why?" but just doing what she's told. She knew it wasn't her place to ask questions. She was doing her best and didn't understand why her mother yelled at her even though she did all she was supposed to. But all she could do was cry into her pillow, hoping that the Witch didn't find out.

As Mirjam got older, the dreams changed. She would often have to run away or hide from some mysterious force in her nightmares, but she forgot what she was running from. She didn't like sleeping anymore, tired of never ending races, so she would stay up late reading or watching movies. One night, she noticed that she couldn't fall asleep, even though she was really tired. It happened the next night and the night after. She felt exhausted during the day and started making mistakes at work. She didn't like mistakes, People get angry when you're not doing what you're supposed to do, so she started getting frustrated at herself. She went to the doctor, who gave her sleeping pills, but they made her very groggy during the day. So her work performance didn't improve. She started feeling angry, really angry inside, and couldn't understand where it was coming from. On one hand, anger brought adrenaline, the need to act that she was missing, but her body was so tired that she just couldn't do anything to burn this strong force with any activity.

Mirjam didn't notice when the anger transformed into anxiety, stronger and stronger as the time passed, until one day she woke up with an overwhelming feeling of fear, like she's never experienced before.

"I'm going crazy," - she thought. "I'm losing my mind and I'm going to end up in a mental institution." This though terrified her even more. She saw herself being locked up in a white room, tied down to a bed, with doctors giving her courses of electric shocks. As the vision enveloped her, she felt her heart beating like crazy. Her breathing became shallow and fast and the room started spinning. The fear was stronger and stronger and she felt darkness coming upon her. "I'm dying," was her last thought before she passed out.

She was awakened by her roommate - Kate, who found her lying on the kitchen floor when she got home from work. Mirjam told Kate what happened, surprised to still be alive. Kate called the ambulance and Mirjam spent the next couple of days in the hospital getting tested for all possible diseases. She was released with a clean bill of health and anti-anxiety medication in her pocket. She knew she should've been happy, but the news didn't really explain what happened to her and how to deal with it.

Mirjam spent a couple of weeks home researching her symptoms and found a lot information about anxiety and panic disorders and drugs that doctors prescribed for it. She had enough wits left in her to understand that pills cannot fix everything. So she kept on looking. She read medical websites, downloaded books on anxiety, and tried out some breathing exercises recommended by her counselor. The last one seemed to be helping, so she changed her course of searching toward natural medicine. One day, she came upon a word that changed everything. The word was AWARENESS.

She started being mindful of what was going on in her mind. As she watched her thoughts, she saw how they affected her actions. As she listened to her inner voice, it brought her backwards in time, step by step, to that tiny little girl afraid of the bad old Witch. And then she stepped onto the road to freedom.

4.

CHOOSE AWARENESS

"Knowing others is wisdom, knowing yourself is Enlightenment."
~ Tao Tzu ~

I've mentioned awareness few times already, but this is such an important part of your choice-making process that it deserves its own chapter. Actually, to be able to make conscious choices, you first need to be aware of what choices you've been making so far with your thoughts, words, and actions. Awareness is the first step into living your life the way you want it.

WHAT IS AWARENESS?

Awareness is an ability to perceive, to see, to feel, to know, and to realize what is happening around you and within you. What we are most concerned with here is being aware of one-self, in other words, *self-awareness.*

Being aware, being conscious of what you think, what you do, what you feel, and *why* you feel it and do it is so important that it should be taught in primary schools! Awareness gives you power over your own life. If you are conscious of what you think - you can change the thoughts that don't serve you well. If you're aware of what you feel - you can explore these feelings and understand your inner drives and motivations. If you realize what actions you take - you can choose to make changes and act in your best interest. Everything starts with awareness. Your journey of self-discovery and taking back the power to make choices starts with awareness. You cannot make choices if you're not aware that you are making them at each and every moment of your life!

Usually, we work on an autopilot. There are many functions of our bodies and mind that we do automatically. It is our subconscious mind that controls those automatic functions and responses. Subconsciousness controls your basic needs.

The inner mind also runs all the programs that you have ever learned in life. When you were a baby learning to walk, you had to think of each movement of your legs and arms and control your balance to be able to take that one step. Then, after you did it a few times and practiced some more, it became a habit. Now you don't have to think about each step as you're walking. It's the same with driving a car. Do you remember how hard it was at first? You had to consciously remember all the separate steps that driving required - steering, changing gears, pushing the right pedals, looking left and right, checking your mirrors, watching the distance, the traffic signs, the other cars ... So many things to do at once! Do you even realize that you're doing all those things while you're driving now? Probably not. You've learned it, you've practiced it, and now it became automatic. You can drive and listen to music and maybe talk to your passengers at the same time. Subconscious controls all the movements while you concentrate on just staying safe and enjoying your journey.

Your thoughts and your feelings and many responses work on the same principles. At some point in life, usually in our childhood and teenage years you learned what to think about yourself and the world. You looked at your parents and saw how relationships worked. You listened to your teachers as they told you about social standards and requirements. You went through situations with your friends and family and learned which of your reactions give you people's approval and which take it away.

If your parents were very conservative, disapproved and punished you for expressing opinions other than theirs, you learned that speaking your mind gets you in trouble. So in your own immature mind, a thought was born: *"It's not ok to speak my mind. It doesn't matter what I think. It only matters what other people think."* This thought, if practiced for a while, becomes a habit, becomes automatic. So now that you're an adult, you don't even realize that you're thinking this particular thought every time you talk to others and as a result you disregard what you actually think and agree with their point of view. It's automatic.

If you were bullied at school for being fat, you started thinking that you're ugly. You've repeated this thought very often and it has become automatic too. Let's say you started watching your diet very closely and exercising excessively. You lost the extra weight, but the thought of being ugly remained. You started comparing yourself to others and getting on even stricter diets, not seeing the point when you actually became so thin that it started affecting your health. It all started with a thought that became habitual.

It gets even weirder than that! What if your mother wasn't very affectionate to you, but when you got sick, she brought you soup, medicines, and made sure that you're warm and feeling well? The mind of a child created an association of being sick and receiving affection and love. Your subconscious mind took that thought and made it seem necessary to get sick more and more often, in order to receive your mother's attention. That's how you were getting the love and affection every child craves. Now as an adult, you're very often catching colds and flu, wondering why is it that nobody in your office caught this bug, but you did? Again? Even if you don't live with your mother anymore, the thought of getting attention and love when being sick remains and takes power not only over your mind - but your body, as well!

Mind is very powerful and we don't know the extent of its mysterious forces. We do know, though, that thoughts that are thought for a while become beliefs and habits, hidden in our inner minds, becoming programs that our subconscious runs in an automatic mode. These thoughts that we don't even know we have create blueprints of our behavior, our choices, our lives! That's why it's so important to become aware of those thoughts. So we can consciously take off the blindfold of these automatic beliefs and start making conscious choices!

❧❧❧❧❧

CONSCIOUS VERSUS SUBCONSCIOUS MIND

Let's start by saying that the mind never stops working. NEVER. The mind is on 24 hours a day, 7 days a week, 365 days a year.

When you're awake, your conscious mind is turned on. It's in control when you do any intentional, voluntary actions like moving your hand to scratch your nose or picking up a cup to drink you tea. Any action you do on purpose, while you're aware of doing it, is controlled by the conscious mind. The conscious mind thinks logically and reasons. When you're making a decision whether to go on holidays, it's your conscious mind that weighs pros and cons, makes sure that you can afford it, and that your plans are doable. When you're reading these words, it's your conscious mind that registers the sentences and thinks of the meaning of them and further - runs my words by your value and belief system to check if they make sense to you. As it is a "gate-keeper" of your mind, it makes sure the content you're presented with matches your belief system that I'm not trying to trick you into thinking something that's not true to you. If someone criticizes you or calls you names, your conscious mind protects you in a way, as well - it checks with your belief system whether these words are true and if you don't believe them, it just discards them as only someone's opinion of you.

Even though this "inner judge" that the conscious mind is, is supposed to work for you safety and benefit, it's because of that particular feature of consciousness that it's so hard to change habits or unlearn thoughts and beliefs while in conscious state. Many smokers have found that out the hard way, when trying to quit the habit. Just because you tell yourself that it's not good for your health, it costs way too much, and it makes you smell bad is not enough to keep your will so strong to actually quit it for good. It's because you've learned to smoke a long time ago and have your reasons to do it that are protected by the ironclad fence of the conscious mind.

The subconscious mind, on the other hand, is the part of your mind that is always on, whether you're awake, asleep, or daydreaming. This is the part that controls all your involuntary actions. It makes sure that you're breathing and that your heart beats to pump the blood in your body all the time, so you stay alive. It tells you when you're hungry or tired.

There are many things happening to you and around you as you go through your daily life. Consciously, you're remembering only some of these things, the ones that are important to you at the moment. All the other things go directly into your subconscious mind to the storeroom of ALL that you ever experienced. All your memories are put away into the drawers of subconscious cabinets. All that you've ever read, saw, heard, smelled, and experienced is stored away. Not only the memories, but the feelings that go with them stay in your subconsciousness. So that's why sometimes you get the nice feeling passing by the bakery and then you remember you mom's Sunday muffins. Usually you don't think about it, but the memory is still there, along with the feeling. And it all can be triggered by a sensory stimulus connected to this experience in the past.

Same as the nice memories stay in your inner mind, the unpleasant ones are there as well. Let's say that you got bitten by a dog when you were five years old as you were walking in the park with your dad, eating strawberry ice-cream. It probably was traumatic for such a small child, so this memory was stored away almost immediately and locked tightly in the subconscious mind. You don't consciously remember that incident, but for some reason, every time you taste or even smell strawberry ice-cream you get this anxious feeling in your stomach ... Just because you don't remember the incident, it doesn't mean it's not there. It shows itself in the form of feeling or a symptom. How many people in the world have illnesses of "unknown" origins that cannot be treated with medications? Irritable bowel syndrome is a reaction to specific situations for some people because there is something in their inner mind that connects this current situation with some situation from the past that caused them the same reaction.

The subconscious mind doesn't have the reasoning ability of the conscious mind, it only stores information and takes them as true, then makes you act based on these stored data.

It's the same when it comes to the beliefs and habits. As I explained before, beliefs and habits are thoughts and actions that were performed many, many, *many* times and got learned and then put away into the subconsciousness as one of its automatic software programs. The subconscious mind doesn't think whether these habits or thoughts are true or beneficial to you. It takes that if they exist, they must be for your own good, and just performs them over and over again. Below the threshold of your consciousness, your awareness and without your choice in the matter.

The good way to explain the consciousness and subconsciousness is to imagine an iceberg in the ocean. There is a tip of it above the water that we can see. But below the water there is even bigger part of it, hidden from our sight, unless we take a dive in.

The point of practicing awareness is to realize what is below the surface while still being above the water.

❧❧❧

PRACTICING AWARENESS

Learning awareness is just like any other thing you've ever learned in life. It takes time and practice. But it also gets easier as you go along and with time it will be as natural to you as breathing.

Did you know that it takes only twenty-one days to learn or unlearn a habit?

Start with observing the world around you. When you wake up in the morning, take your time; instead of rushing out of bed and getting ready to work in a hurry. Maybe set up your alarm fifteen minutes early? Get up and go to the window. Look outside, see what the weather is like. Is the sun shining? What does it illuminate? What are the colors outside? Are there any people, plants, animals? If you can, open the window and take a deep breath of fresh air. Really *feel it* filling up your lungs. Are there any smells in the air? Maybe flowers are blooming or there is a bakery close by and you can smell the fresh bread? Then stretch your body, maybe do couple of easy exercises, simple bending down really stretches your back muscles and gets the energy going in your body while relaxing it at the same time.

When getting ready, take your time. Feel the texture of your face cream between your fingers before applying it to your face. Or touch the shaving foam and notice how funny this white whipped substance filled with air feels on your skin... When picking out your clothes, really look at the colors, touch the material, and just notice the sensations.

Then it's time for breakfast - never skip breakfast! It's not only important for nourishment and giving your body energy for the day, but it also lets you get your thoughts together and concentrate before setting off to your daily routine. In our busy times, mealtimes have been reduced to just filling up your stomach to kill the feeling of hunger. Often, we just stuff it with whatever is easy to grab on the go, not even noticing the quality of the food that is supposed to keep our bodies strong and healthy. Think what food you're putting on your plate. Is it natural and valuable? What nutrients does it bring into your system? Really take time to chew your food. Take smaller bites. Taste each bite, feel the texture of foods in your mouth. It's not only for awareness and getting pleasure out of eating, but it's also one of the best ways to stay slim! It takes about twenty minutes for your brain to receive the signals from your stomach that it's full. By eating fast, you actually eat too much and set yourself up to gain extra pounds.

Before the fast-food era, meals were not only for eating, but they were important times of getting together with family and friends, spending time as a group and enjoying the moment of connection. Make your mealtimes important part of your family routine. If you can't do it for each meal, at least set up few days a week for eating together. Eat slowly, engage in conversation, and notice how much fun eating can be!

As you go through your day, driving to work, walking to the shop, having coffee with a friend, or just taking a walk - keep your eyes open. You don't need to stare at your feet as you walk, you already know that your subconscious is taking care of making each step properly. Look around you. See the people you pass by. What are they wearing? What do their faces say? Where are they going? Look at the buildings. What colors are they? Are there any decorations on the façade? Any flowers on the balconies? Open your other senses too. Listen to the sounds. Did you notice that each car makes a different sound? That there are owls living on that tree near the bus stop? That the clerk at your supermarket has this really soft, kind voice? Then as you sit on your couch, relaxing after your day, touch the pillows, the cover, is it soft or hard? Take off your shoes and let the dog lick your feet. Feel the sensations all around you.

As you live your days, experiencing them with all your senses, you will train yourself to open up to the world around you and living in it more consciously.

At the same time, you can start working at being aware of your body. As you're sitting and reading these words right now, move your toes. Turn your ankles in circles to the right and then to the left. Stretch your legs and tighten your muscles. And then loosen them up. Tighten again and let go. Notice the feeling or tension and relaxation. Then move your attention to your stomach. Squeeze it in and push it out. Notice the difference in sensations. Check with your stomach for the feeling of hunger. Is there rumbling in your tummy? Now take a deep breath and feel your chest move up and down as you breathe out. Take a couple more breaths and feel the air in your lungs. Think of all the oxygen that it brings to each and every one of your body cells. Imagine that for a moment. See the particles of oxygen travelling into your bloodstream, going to this cell or another one, maybe to a cell located in your arm or in your ear. As you think of the blood, hear your heartbeat, pumping this blood in your veins. Is it fast or slow? ...

Now move your attention to your neck. Is it tight or lose? Move your head left and right, roll it around slowly and notice how the tension in the neck is being released with each movement of your head. Take your left hand now and touch the skin on your right arm. Gently first. Is it tickly? Then scratch it a bit. What is the sensation? Now look at your hands. Do you wear any rings, bracelets, maybe a watch? What do they feel like on your skin? Stretch out your fingers then tighten them into a fist. Then touch your face with your fingers. What is the sensation on your fingers? What is the sensation on your face? Shift your attention to your mouth. Is it moist or dry? Touch your teeth with your tongue. What do you feel? Now concentrate on the sounds around you for a moment. Then cover your ears with your hands. What can you hear now? How did the sounds change? Now look in front of you. Look to the left, then to the right. Look down at yourself. And finally, close your eyes. Is everything black or can you see anything in your inner mind's eye?

Doing this exercise daily, even parts of it is a great way to develop the awareness of your body and to connect with the fact that you exist. You are physically here. Your body is here. And your mind is here so it can observe and experience your body. You are here. You exist.

Further awareness of your body can be developed through different activities. I strongly recommend starting exercise practice such as Yoga or Tai-Chi. Or anything else you enjoy doing. Just *notice* what your body feels like as you're doing these activities. Pay attention to the movements, to your muscles, to your breath, and to your heartbeat. Connect with your body.

When you notice that you're aware of your surroundings and your body, it's time to shift your attention inwards. Notice how you feel and ask yourself *why* do you feel it?

Each day you're going through many experiences and all those experiences evoke different emotions in you. If you're able to realize what it is that you feel in connection to this experience or another then you can then think about the reason why you feel it and if the emotion doesn't work in your favor - you can decide to change it.

(We will explore the technical process of changing your emotions in Chapter 6).

When you open your eyes in the morning, are you excited about having another amazing day before you or do you dread getting out of bed and going to that "dammed job" again? When you read the morning paper or listen to the news on the radio, do some of them make you sad or angry or you just take from it whatever is directly connected with you and disregard the rest? When you're at work dealing with a difficult client, do you get impatient and want to tell them to "just go to hell" or maybe you feel compassion for the person who is so unhappy that he feels he needs to take his frustrations out on others? When your boss makes a comment about your performance, do you feel discouraged, angry, or maybe depressed, or do you just take it as a constructive criticism that you can learn from and feel grateful? What about if you argue with your partner about something silly, do you get down easily or feel really mad or do you concentrate on the feeling of deep love you have for him and turn the argument into something funny? What if someone on the street asked you for money and you refused, do you feel guilty or do you feel compassion for the person but accept the fact that you cannot help them at the moment? What if you need to speak out at a meeting, do you feel enormous anxiety, or do you feel confidence and joy at the opportunity to voice your ideas? At times, you may just feel crappy all day for no apparent reason or you may just be joyful all day for no reason as well.

Check with yourself often everyday your feelings by simply taking a breath and asking: How do I feel in this moment? How do I feel about this situation? How do I feel about this person?

No need to question your happiness, joy, or love, although being thankful for all the things that make you happy is a way of prolonging that feeling. But if you feel emotion such as sadness, guilt, anger, anxiety, rage, shame, envy, irritation, disappointment, or disgust, you may want to question yourself as for why you feel the way you feel. Remember that feelings and emotions are your guidance system and they point out whether you're living by the beliefs that work for your benefit or not. And that being aware of how you feel is the first step towards creating a positive change in your life.

✸❦✸

Are you aware of what you're thinking, saying, and doing? If you've been practicing awareness of your body and your feelings, it will be easier for you to follow up with the next step, which is awareness of thoughts and actions.

The biggest enemy of awareness is rushing. If you're living on the fast lane, you do many things on an autopilot. You say things without thinking, you do things on an impulse. Slow down and give yourself time to take a breath. Even just one deep breath before answering a question or taking a step makes a huge difference. Those few seconds are enough time for you to examine what it is that you're about to say or do and whether the thought that you have in your head is true and beneficial for you. To realize what it is that you're actually thinking, what you're putting out there with your words and actions. To be aware of yourself. So next time, if a friend asks you about your day and you're about to say how horrible it was, just take a breath and think - was it really so terrible or am I just concentrating on that one comment I overheard about myself that made me feel bad? Or next time you want to grab another Snicker's bar from the shelf, take a breath and question - am I really hungry or am I just trying to make myself feel better with extra sugar?

Once you're aware I can promise you that your life will take on a whole new meaning. You will realize how great of a power you have inside yourself to choose how you interact with the world and with yourself and to make deliberate choices that will create a life you've always dreamed of!

"Awareness is empowering."
~ Rita Wilson ~

Miracle of Well-Being

Someone said yoga will bring you serenity. One summer, Mirjam decided to test this theory, especially since she always promised herself to start exercising. She tried running and gym before, but she got bored with these easily and found ten thousand excuses why she couldn't exercise that day or that week. Or the next one. And the one after that. The problem was that she needed something deeper than simple weight lifting or running without destination. She needed exercise with a soul.

And so there was yoga.

It looked easy enough, what is couple of stretches? But the first class proved Mirjam wrong. It wasn't easy at all! She felt muscles in her body that she didn't even know existed. She found out that she had no balance. And the worst part was breathing. In as you go into a pose and out as you go out of it. She tried breathing deep and slow, but the more she concentrated on the breath, the more shallow and faster it became. At one the point, she felt that if she will not think about breathing, the breathing will stop. How absurd, Breathing is an automatic function of the body and cannot stop even if you faint! Well, Mirjam did faint a couple of times, probably out of the hyperventilation she got herself into, but knowing her, we may assume she just wanted to prove the theory right.

Mirjam wanted to be fit and serene. She like the way her body felt after the yoga class. So she decided to first learn how to breathe right.

5.

CHOOSE BREATHING

Breath is one of the most powerful forms of healing. People of the Orient have appreciated the art of deep breathing throughout the centuries and included breathwork in their spiritual and healing practices, such as meditation, tai-chi, yoga, or qi-gong. The results - they live longer than any other cultures and remain healthy until old age.

We, living in the Western "civilized" societies, along with other important workings of the body, mind, and spirit, have forgotten how important breathing is. Just think - a person can survive three weeks without food, three days without water, but only three minutes without air... We start our lives with that "first breath" and give out the "last breath" as we leave this world. Breath brings in the life-supporting oxygen into all cells of our bodies through the blood stream. Without it, our hearts will not beat, our brains will not think, and our organs will not support us through their complicated processes and functions.

Breath also brings in the life force energy into our bodily temples. If we take fast shallow breaths, that energy is very low, there's barely enough of it for our survival. What about the vitality and strength to be the best we can be and experience our lives fully? Don't we need energy for that too? Deep breathing connects you to the Universe around you, to its energy, among other things. So as you breathe, consciously draw in the life force energy into your body with the air you take it and allow it to fill you up. This connection to the Universe can be maintained ALL THE TIME, as long as you breathe! And you breathe continuously, don't you?

Deep breathing also creates stillness of the mind. If you concentrate completely on the breathing, everything else disappears. People look for ways to meditate, to "clear their minds", but they have the proper tool with them all along! Concentrate on each breath you take, only on the action of taking the air in and letting it out. You will be surprised how easily you forget these thoughts that were racing through your head, the problems you were trying to solve, and the worries that were taking your joy away. All that will be left is the breath, peace, and stillness. And in this state of mind your awareness awakens. Suddenly, as you are aware of your breathing, you become aware of yourself. You become aware of your feelings and what were these feelings again? Yes - the first step to understanding your thoughts, your beliefs, and your actions. The first step to making conscious choices for yourself!

Use that amazing tool that you were born with and breathe your way to your own freedom!

PROPER BREATHING

You've been breathing all your life, but have you been doing it the right way?

Well, anyway you breathe you get some oxygen into your body, of course. You're still alive, after all. But in order to get just the right amount, you must know *how* to breathe.

If you've ever had singing or choir classes, you're probably aware of a thing called the "diaphragm". It's a muscle that extends across the bottom of the ribcage and separates the upper "thoracic" cavity of your body (heart, lungs and ribs) from the lower "abdominal" cavity. Its main function is to support respiration - in simple words: breathing. As you inhale, the diaphragm contracts, enlarging your chest cavity, which in turn creates suction that draws air into your lungs. When the diaphragm relaxes, the air is pushed out form the lungs during the exhalation.

There are two types of inhaling, according to how you direct your diaphragm muscles during the process. When the central tendon of the diaphragm is still and the lower ribs are mobile, the contraction expands chest cavity laterally and upwards, moving the ribs to the sides. This is what we'd call "chest breathing" and it's more shallow than the second kind, as the ribs are not very flexible, being made of bone and can only expand to a certain point. When the lower ribs are still and the central tendon of the diaphragm is mobile, the contraction of this muscle expands the chest cavity downwards, towards the pelvis. This is called "belly breathing" or "deep breathing" and it's what you should be aiming for while doing your breathing exercises. Belly breathing allows for more air to come into your lungs, as the chest cavity enlarges much more downwards then to the sides, due to the organs being much softer and more flexible than the ribs.

Interesting fact - men usually breathe with their belly, while women use their chest. So it's a bit easier for men as their diaphragm is already used to expanding downwards, while women have to learn it. But do not fret women - you remember how long it takes to create a habit? Yes, only twenty-one days!

So how to breathe properly using your belly breathing?

Try this right now: lie down or sit down with your back straight. Put your right hand on your chest and the left one on your stomach. Inhale. Which hand moved? If it's the right one - you're breathing with your chest. Now do the next breath consciously.

As you inhale, push your stomach out, so your left hand moves outwards. The right hand shouldn't have moved at all. Easy, isn't it?

But exhaling is just as important as inhaling, to push all the stale, used air out of your lungs. So as you breathe out, suck your stomach muscles inwards and see your left hand moving inwards. Now try it again, slowly. Inhale - push the stomach out, exhale - suck the stomach in. And as you breathe, allow your breathing to be slow and thorough. Fill up your lungs as much as you can in this deep slow inhalation, then slowly let out all the air from the lungs.

This simple exercise will teach your muscles to expand downwards, allowing you to take fuller, deeper breaths and in time will become a habit for you.

When I first started practicing this deep breathing technique, I put post-its with the word BREATHE all around the house and some even at work. They were reminders to stop for a moment and take three deep breaths. Not only did I learn the technique quickly and easily, but it also helped me relax in the crazy rush of my daily life.

~◦❦◦~

BREATHING EXERCISES

To get the benefits of deep breathing, you don't really need that much time or a special place to practice. I prefer to do it in the mornings as a part of my yoga routine and in the evenings as an introduction to my meditation. But the exercises can also be done on your coffee break at work, while on a bus, or during a walk in the park. Basically, any time you can find is good, as long as you practice at least once a day. Remember that you're not used to deep breathing yet, so if you get dizzy, reduce pressure during the exhalation. People with pre-existing breathing disorders should check with their doctor before starting any routine and modify exercises according to their tolerance.

Breathing Exercise 1

To clear out stale air in the lower lung area.
(3-7 breaths 2 times a day)

* Place chin against chest.
* Keep mouth closed.
* Inhale through the nose and tilt head back slowly on inhalation.
* Exhale slowly through the mouth and tilt head forward on exhalation.
* As you exhale, push air out through your teeth to produce hissing sound.

Breathing Exercise 2

To sharpen the senses and willpower.
(3-7 breaths 3 times a day)

* Empty lungs completely.
* Slowly inhale through the nose and fully expand lungs during the inhalation.
* Tightly purse lips as if to whistle.
* Blow air out very slowly under pressure during the exhalation.
* Empty lungs completely.

Breathing Exercise 3

To energize and revitalize the body.
(10 breaths 3 times a day)

* Breathe in and out through your nose.
* Inhale from deep in your abdomen.
* Inhale for 1 count.
* Hold for 4 counts.
* Exhale for 2 counts.

Breathing Exercise 4

To strengthen your energy. Also heats the body from inside.
(as needed)

* Breathe in and out through your nose very fast for 1 minute.
* Inhale for 1 count and exhale for 1 count - it's just like the dog's panting, only through your nose.

Breathing Exercise 5

Prana breathing - connecting with the Earth and Heaven energies and bringing them into your system.
(5 to 10 breaths from each direction as needed)

* Imagine that there is a tube running from the ground, through your body (straight up your spine) and coming out through your head (see diagram). This tube - "pranic tube" is empty inside and connects you with the Earth and Heaven.
* As you inhale, breathe up into the pranic tube from the Earth, drawing the Earth's energy into the tube.
* Hold your breath for a moment as you concentrate on the energy gathered in the pranic tube
* Exhale with audible sigh and as you do that, see the energy from the pranic tube spreading all around your body.
* Now as you inhale, breathe down from above the head into the pranic tube, drawing in Heaven's energy into the tube.

* Hold your breath for a moment as you concentrate on the energy gathered in the pranic tube.
* Exhale with audible sigh and as you do that, see the energy from the pranic tube spreading all around your body.
* Do this five to ten times until you clearly sense a flow of energy into the pranic tube.

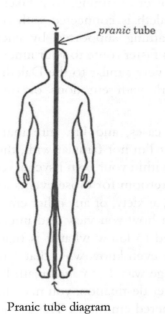

pranic tube

Pranic tube diagram

❧⊙〜⊙⊙〜⊙❧

BREATHWORK EMOTIONAL RELEASE

Additional to concentration, relaxation, and energy work, breathwork has been used in many cultures for spiritual awakening and emotional healing. Techniques such as Daleth Breathwork, Holotropic Breathwork, or Rebirthing through deep connective breathing allow person to enter a different state of consciousness, a very deep trance-like state that connects one to his old traumas and emotional blocks and facilitates their release. I have tried Rebirthing, but as helpful as it was, I found Daleth Breathwork to be a much faster and stronger process. Although the breathing technique is similar in both cases, rebirthing allows for gentler, slower breathing, so it takes much longer to achieve the results. Daleth is connected with old shamanic practices of fast deep breathing supported by energetic drum music and creates a much faster route to your inner destinations. Holotropic Breathwork is very similar to the Daleth kind, but includes more conscious work with emotions or traumas found during the process.

In the above cases, and I'm sure that there are more similar techniques that I'm not familiar with, the breath guides you on a journey deep within your own psyche, searching the labyrinths of your inner storeroom for those events and situations that caused you pain, hurt, anxiety, or any other emotions so strong that they had impact on how you view and interact with the world now. You don't need to know what it is that you're looking for, you probably don't even know what that synthesizing event for your current blockage was. Let your breath be your GPS. When your reach your inner destination, you need to allow yourself to let go of all that gathered emotions. This is the route to freedom from your past, the way to regain your free will to choose for yourself, instead of letting your old barriers and beliefs choose for you. Once the barriers are released and healed, which make take a good few sessions, depending on how deep they're hidden, breathwork can facilitate spiritual evolvement and connection with your Higher Self.

Such breathwork is usually done with an assistance of experienced therapist or guide, as one may not be able to handle these deep emotional releases on his own. But there are also more gentle ways to facilitate emotional healing with the help of breath that you can practice on your own.

❧◦◦◦◦❧

"HEALING THE FEELING" TECHNIQUE

This technique combines visualization with breathing. You need to be already familiar with belly breathing and comfortable enough with it to be able to do it while directing your concentration onto visualizations. You may need to work with the same feeling a few times until it heals and I'd recommend starting with the easier ones, leaving the ones that you've been holding on to for a while, until you're a bit more experienced with this technique.

* Choose a feeling/emotion that you want to transform or heal.
* Close your eyes and pinpoint where in your body you feel this emotion.
* What color is that emotion?
* What color will it be when it's healed?
* Now feel the emotion and see its color in the part of your body where it resides.
* Start taking deep breaths, inhale through your nose, and exhale through your mouth, a bit faster than you usually would breathe and as you breathe *really* feel the emotion and see its color intensely.
* When the emotion is very intense, imagine that with each exhale, the color and the emotion is leaving your body. Breathe it out until you don't see the color or feel the emotion anymore.

* If you have problems releasing the feeling you can imagine that as you inhale, the golden healing air enters your body and dissolves the color and the emotion until it's no more.
* Return to your regular breathing.
* Check the part of your body where the emotion previously was. See its new color. Add feelings of peace, relief, and joy to this color. Start taking deep slow belly breaths now and allow this new color and warm positive emotions to spread all around your body and even come out of your body, surrounding you in a soft shiny bright cocoon of positivity.

"All the principles of heaven and earth are living inside you. Life itself is truth, and this will never change. Everything in heaven and earth breathes. Breath is the thread that ties creation together. "
~ Morihei Ueshiba ~

Miracle of Doing it Anyway

They say "if there's a will, there's a way." Sometimes finding the way can last centuries. At least that's what Mirjam thought.

She recently learned to recognize the inner voices that have guided her all her life, not always to her best possible future. There was a voice of her mother in her head telling her to always listen to others and obey their wishes. There was a voice of her father warning her to stay exactly where she is, as the unknown was too dangerous for her. And the voices of her teachers threatening that she is not smart enough or hard-working enough to achieve anything important in life. Then the voices of her jealous friends laughing at her couple of extra pounds or messy hair, calling her ugly. There was a voice of her ex-boyfriend telling her that he will love her only if she will be his maid. And, finally, her own inner judge that contained all the other voices, only run through the most unforgiving filter of all and then magnified by lack of self-esteem.

The inner judge appeared recently with all his mighty presence when she met Kyle. Kyle was just a friend of a friend who they run into at the coffee shop. They all had a very interesting conversation about organic food and she felt a kind of weird connection with that man. Not a thunder from the sky, blinding her with his magnificence. That kind of falling she already knew. But this was something else. They actually talked about what's important to her. Seems that it was important to him too. She left the conversation with loads of new knowledge in her head, excitement in her heart and his telephone number in her pocket. He actually wanted to take her to this new vegetarian restaurant and show her that there are different ways to eat! Not to take her on a date because she was pretty, but he actually liked to talk to her. That was something Mirjam wasn't used to. Sure, she'd had many guys interested in her, but it was mostly a physical attraction that lit up fast and burned out even faster, without ever reaching the place of deeper connection.

So now, as she cramped the napkin with Kyle's number in her hand, the voices spoke. First, softly, they told her that he must be just like any other man she ever knew, who only liked her looks and pretended to be interested in what she said to get her into the sack. They reminded her that she actually wasn't that pretty, getting older now that she was thirty. They also said she wasn't very smart and Kyle probably just asked her out to be nice, as their mutual friend mentioned that she was single. It probably wasn't even his real phone number. The voices recalled her past relationships, when she was used as a maid, cook, housekeeper, babysitter, secretary, teacher, dog walker, personal trainer, counselor, and then a doormat. They warned her that if she trusted again, she would surely get hurt. "Better safe than sorry." So she put Kyle's number deep into her pocket and hasn't called him yet. It's been two weeks now and she knew that if she waited longer it might be too late.

Yes, she heard the voices now. And she knew that they were wrong. But when she heard them, then and there, she just couldn't stop them from affecting her. Her mind, her intelligence explained why the voices spoke in such ways and she understood now. But she just couldn't shut them up!

Mirjam really liked Kyle. So she did all that she could at the moment. She heard the voices, felt the fear, but she picked up the phone and rang him anyway.

"Hello?" - she heard Kyle's deep voice on the other end.

"Hi, it's Mirjam, not sure if you remember me..." - she started hesitantly.

"Of course I do! I'm so glad you called, Mirjam! I though you lost my number ... So how about that dinner?"

6.

CHOOSE THE POSITIVE

So let's say you've practiced breathing and awakening your awareness for a few weeks now and you are able to distinguish the thoughts that you are thinking. So what's the point of all this self-awareness that you experience more and more each day? The awareness gives you the power to choose, to deliberately decide what you're thinking, to create the life of your dreams through your thoughts.

Remember that autopilot that your mind was running on? Well, now that you know what you're thinking, it's time to turn that automatic system OFF! Take back the control over your thoughts and choose the ones that are better for you. The ones that bring you closer to the kind of life that you were dreaming of. Remember - it is your choice what you think. You can choose to keep believing these negative old patterns, that are the voice of judgment or guilt in your head, or you can shout out:

"ENOUGH! I've let some old lies run my life for way too long! I take my power back NOW! I choose to CHOOSE my thoughts."

You've been used to thinking the same negative, sabotaging thoughts for years. But now you can catch them quickly as they pass through your mind, just like a frog catches a fly, in an instant. How do you do that?

꧁꧂

EMOTIONAL GUIDANCE SYSTEM

First of all, use your Emotional Guidance System.

As I've told you before, your emotions are not just inner feelings that pop up from nowhere. They are important part of your inner being, letting you know of the level of life enjoyment that you're currently experiencing.

We are meant to be happy, to live life exploring this material world and building it in accordance with our vision of happiness. Some life experiences, such as loss of a loved one or sickness are bound to create feelings of unhappiness or sadness. One might feel guilty if he did something against the law or treated another in an unfair way. If there is a genuine reason for the feeling, if the feeling is a response to something that happened, then this feeling is just a part of that particular experience. Blocking those feelings would impair this experience and you might not receive the full lesson that was there for you to learn. So go ahead, feel those feelings. Feel them to the fullest. But then - just let them go.

Unpleasant experiences are bound to happen, as in order to learn things, we need to experience them. We've set up these situations and lessons long before we came down to the Earth into this incarnation. We may not be aware of the reasons for these painful things as they are happening. Only in time we will learn what they were truly about. Therefore, there is no reason to deem situations "bad" and to disregard negative feelings as unneeded. They are part of who we are, part of being a human, part of experiencing life, which is not to say that clinging to sadness or guilt is healthy and constructive for one's life. FEEL the emotion and LET IT GO.

The problem arises when we feel emotions that are not justified by the experience or we keep the unpleasant feelings for so long that they become constant part of our lives, thus inhibiting us from moving forward. A teenager who wakes up every morning for weeks feeling sad is not just reacting to some situation. A woman who feels guilty every time she says "no" to someone doesn't feel it because she commits an unlawful act. A man who reacts with anger when someone asks him to move to the side and let them through has not been violated. These are the feelings that show us that there is something wrong going on in our subconsciousness, that there is some thought or belief or program that tells us to react with such feeling, regardless of the need for such emotion or such intensity. These are the automatic programs that have been choosing for you and now you are in a position to change them.

✺

THE "STOP" TECHNIQUE

I didn't say, choosing differently was easy, but you're already far ahead with being aware of what you feel and think. Now I will give you another tool that will help you change the automatic thoughts into the ones that you choose.

I call it the STOP Technique, which stands for:

Stop,
Think,
Opt for
Positive.

Whenever you feel emotions such as: sadness, anxiety, anger, guilt, rage, shame, resentment, jealousy, grudge, despair, isolation,

87

disgust, disappointment, or fear I'd like to ask you to STOP and follow the steps below. Look in appendix for a Stop Technique Spreadsheet that will help you examine the situation. With practice you will be able to do it quickly in your head, when the need arises.

1. *Stop.* Close your eyes, take a deep breath, and imagine a huge Stop sign in front of your inner eye. The sign is telling you to stop your feelings and racing thoughts for just a moment. It may be helpful to imagine your emotions and thoughts as a mist of many different colors that moves in the air and suddenly stops and stands still when it reaches the Stop sign. This is done in order to gently remove yourself from the intensity of what is going on inside you, in order to examine it from a perspective of an observer.

2. *Think.* Examine the emotion like a detective. Ask yourself questions:

* Why am I having this emotion, this feeling?
* What is happening in my life right now that may cause this feeling?

If there is a situation that causes it, then follow up with the next questions:

* Is my emotional reaction proportionate to this situation?
* If this situation happened to someone else, would they have similar reaction or not?
* If my friend or family member reacted in this way to the same situation, what would I tell them?

If, on the other hand, there is no experience in your current life that justifies your emotion or if the emotion is overly strong comparing to what happened, ask yourself:

* What is the thought behind this emotion?

Take the first thought that pops into your mind and examine it:

* Is this thought actually true?
* What proofs do I have that it is true?
* What proofs do I have that it is not true?
* What positives is this thought bringing into my life?
* What negatives is this thought bringing into my life?
* How would I feel without this thought?
*Do I still want this thought?

3. **Opt for Positive.** This is the key moment of experiencing your true power - the Power of Choice. You've examined the feeling, you've found the thought and if you examined it closely, you've more than likely realized that you don't want this thought anymore, as it's not bringing anything good into your life experience. Now it's time to choose the positive one.

Ask yourself:

* What is the positive thought, opposite to what I was thinking thus far, that will benefit my life?

The most important part of this step is to remember to think *positive* thoughts. I've said it before and will repeat it many more times. Don't say what you don't want, but what you *do* want. Saying what you do not want keeps you in the negative space of imagining your worst nightmares, therefore, making them come true. You've probably often thought something like: *"I don't want to get sick"* when people around you were sneezing and coughing and you ended up with the flu. Or *"I don't want to be alone"* at the party and somehow spent it standing in the corner by yourself. Or even worse, worrying about a recession and losing your job, wishing *"I don't want to get fired"* and ending up exactly where you didn't want to be. This is because you were concentrating on what you didn't want in life instead of what you want, and you're probably aware of how powerful your thoughts are by now. They create things.

"A man is but the product of his thoughts what he thinks, he becomes."
~ Mahatma Gandhi ~

Do a little exercise right now, just to see for yourself how powerful your mind is. Close your eyes and think about your best friend. See his face in front of you, all the details, eyes, nose, hair. See him or her smiling at you. Now, while you do that, I want you to please, please, *please* do not think about flying elephants. Under no circumstances I want to think about, imagine or see flying elephants. What just happened? Did you just see flying elephants in your mind's eye? I did tell you *not* to think about them! The mind doesn't distinguish if you say "no" it just imagines whatever you think about. So be mindful of your thoughts and only think of what you want!

Just to be completely sure that you've chosen the positive thought, ask yourself:

* How does this thought make me feel?

If your answer is: happy, joyful, excited, free, relaxed, peaceful, etc., then this is the right thought for you.

Once you have your absolutely fabulous positive thought, you need to make sure to write it into your inner computer system. Write it down on a piece of paper. Put it in your wallet, write it on your cell phone on your computer screen, put it on a post-it on your mirror, fridge or at wall at workplace. Read it often and repeat it many times in your head and aloud. Make a song about it. Write a poem about it. Do it to the moment when you feel you believe it. The feeling is very important. Remember the Emotional Guidance System? When you feel the thought is true to you, that's when it became an automatic part of you.

The STOP process can be applied to your words and actions, as well. If you become aware that there is something that you often repeatedly say or do, stop and ask yourself: *"Why am I saying or doing this?"* And follow the steps of the technique. I'm sure you will astound yourself with your findings and uncover your inner Power of Choice.

"Once you replace negative thoughts with positive ones, you'll start having positive results."
~ Willie Nelson ~

Miracle of Excitement

It was a lovely sunny Saturday, but Mirjam woke up feeling uneasy or maybe even anxious. She had a day off, but from the time she opened her eyes her thoughts were circling around ten thousand things she needed to do today.

In the last months, she's been creating her art portfolio during the day and working at a café as a waitress in the evening to pay her bills. She didn't have to work today and was really tired, exhausted actually, and all she dreamed about was staying in bed and doing nothing. But that was inappropriate, her inner judge said. "Can't waste precious time and be lazy!" She needed to clean the house, do some food shopping, and then sit down at her computer to work on her website where she wanted to do a showcase of her paintings. And to finish that landscape feature she was painting yesterday. All these were very serious and important matters she just had to deal with.

Even painting, her most beloved passion, was just another errand on her to do list. Somehow, it stopped giving her pleasure since she decided to make it her work instead of just a hobby. She was worried about money - how will she ever be able to support herself if she won't find people to buy her paintings? She had to make her portfolio bigger and more diverse and put it all on the web as soon as possible and then advertise and make phone calls to galleries.

"Oh, man ..." - Mirjam sighed. She was even more tired now from all the thinking and she hasn't even gotten up! And the house is a mess, there's no food in the fridge ...

When did her life stop being fun? Mirjam remembered when she made the important changes in her life not that long ago. She changed her career drastically from being an accountant, which she truly hated, into developing her painting passion into a craftsmanship. Ever since, she started enjoying her life again. She woke up before the alarm rang, excited to be able to do what she loved. She had her evening job and knowing that it was helping her get closer to her dreams made it bearable despite late hours and often unpleasant customers. First months were like a dream come true, but now she realized that she didn't remember the last time she felt that sheer happiness of life. Everything became so serious. So many things to do! The responsibility to make a living and become a respectable artist ...

She felt lost again. She knew she needed to go back to that place where she took the wrong turn and get back to the real reasons why she was painting.

Mirjam picked up the phone and ordered pizza. Pizza for breakfast? ... Who said it wasn't allowed? She slowly got up, looked at the house, which wasn't really as messy as she made herself believe it to be. Waiting for the food to arrive, she opened up the balcony door and took in the lovely smell of morning mist. It really was a lovely day!

When she finished her unusual breakfast, Mirjam put on her old paint-stained clothes and laid down a huge canvas on the floor. She took out the paints, but no brushes this time. She had no idea what she was going to create, but that is what actually awakened her excitement. The journey into the Unknown! With her fingers dipped in red and yellow, she closed her eyes and felt her way around the canvas.

"No peeking" -she reminded herself. This was going to be a surprise. She only opened her eyes a couple of times to choose other colors, then closed them again not to look at the work in progress.

Mirjam felt like a child, playing with the paints with no real plan or purpose. And how fun was that!

She knew this was the piece of the puzzle that she had lost along the way - the child within that needed to have fun in the process of working. And when she looked at the finished masterpiece, she was stunned by the diversity of textures it contained. This was the most interesting picture she painted so far!

Mirjam promised herself to never again forget the needs of her inner child.

And when she sat down to finish her to do list in the evening, it wasn't as unpleasant anymore, as all that morning fun gave her strength and motivation to go on.

7.

CHOOSE YOUR INNER CHILD

Sometimes I wish we could all go back to being children. We were not as knowledgeable then, nor were we doing everything properly, but we had this special kind of wisdom that seems to disappear as we grow up.

Children love life. They are excited just to BE. They get up every morning with a yearning for new experiences, eager to play and explore the world. To a child, the most important thing is to feel good. And they generally do feel good, as it is human nature to be happy. But if something disturbs their enjoyment of life, they don't complain and wallow in sorrow. They look for solutions, for things to make them feel better. If the child is hungry - he will ask for food. If he is tired, he will go to sleep wherever he is (which makes for some pretty funny pictures!). If he is falls down and hurts himself, he will run to his mom and she'll make it all better with a hug and a kiss. Aren't these the best medicines?

Children trust their feelings. Sometimes they meet a person and just don't like them. Not for any special reason, but they do get the "vibe" from that person that they will just not do well together. Parent will most likely make the child "be nice" and interact with that person, but time will prove that the first intuitive response of the child was right and any close relationship with the "unliked" person did not form. Very often, children feel what and who is good for them - if their instincts are not killed by teaching them to disregard their inner voice, that is.

Children act on their feelings. If the child is happy, he will smile. If he's sad, he will cry. If he's mad, he will scream. To the adults, it may seem like they're overacting at times, but do they really? The child will act out the emotion and then let it go. He will not hold it back or hide it, he will not pretend it doesn't exist. But as soon as he expressed it, he will let it go and move on with his day.

Children tend to put all their attention and effort into what they are doing at the moment. If they paint, they will do that with such passion that part of their painting will be on the table and most likely on their clothes too. It does not matter if they have paint in their hair or on their face. They were making a picture, nothing else mattered. If they play theater, they will use props, change their clothes and appearance to fit the role, and add proper voices and gestures. They will put all their spirit into their role. And they won't notice the time passing by. Children live in the present moment and feel it with all their being.

Children have a special kind of sight. They are able to notice small amazing things that are invisible to the adult eye. A little boy will spend hours watching ants build their nest. A little girl will comment on each flower she passes by walking back from school. Children see sunsets, butterflies, and baby birds. They are amazed by all that surrounds them and look at everything as it was the most interesting thing they have ever seen. They look through the eyes of Love.

At last, but not least - children use their imagination *all the time*. A child will look at the cloud and see animals, castles, and stories playing out in the sky. He will see a pattern on the wall that reminds him of labyrinths and an ancient story will be created in his mind. Playing dress up, the child will take on his role so much that he will believe he's actually the brave warrior fighting a mighty dragon. A child can close his eyes and dream of becoming a singer when he grows up and, as he dreams, he feels the excitement of going on stage and performing, hears the crowds cheering, and sees the spotlight. If the child wants a chocolate, he will immediately remember the last time he ate it and imagine what it tasted like to the point that he'll begin to drool.

Yes, we should all be more like the children that we used to be. We actually can awaken the child within us, if we just try a little bit. And this inner child will show us how to play with life and enjoy it in its pure form of unconditional love for all that is.

> *"A grownup is a child with layers on."*
> ~ Woody Harrelson ~

AWAKEN YOUR INNER CHILD

One of the ways to add more fun and joy into your life is by stirring that inner boy or girl you have within. The meditation below helps to awaken that inner child. You can have someone read it to you or record your own voice, play it back, and enjoy! It's best if you relax your body and mind prior to doing the meditation. You can do that by taking deep breaths and concentrating on relaxing each part of your body from top to the bottom.

⸙◦❀◦⸙

INNER CHILD MEDITATION

"Take a deep strong regular breath and allow yourself to relax. As you keep on breathing in this peaceful, regular manner, allow yourself to let go and go deep within yourself.

I want you to imagine now that you are standing on the top of a beautiful hill. When you look down, you can see all different colors on the hillside. There are dark green trees, yellow sunflowers, red poppies, white lilies, light green meadows, and all the way on the bottom you can see dark-blue river slowly flowing through the valley. You can hear birds singing a joyful song and a gentle hum of the water down in the valley. It's a warm summer day, the sun is shining, and it makes your skin warm and it makes the water in the river below glisten and sparkle.

In front of you, there is a path, this path is leading you down the hillside and towards the river. Go down that path now and as you keep on walking slowly and peacefully you feel very happy and very relaxed. As you walk down and down the path, just see all that surrounds you. You're passing the trees and flowers and meadows. There are many beautiful colors all around you and you feel happy and safe just to be here.

In front of you on the path there is an old wall and a metal gate, decorated with mysterious ornaments. There is a sign on the gate saying "Fantasy Land," and you realize now that behind the wall there is a magical kingdom of childhood, filled with fun, laughter, and fantasy. You feel so excited to go on an adventure! When you're ready, you open the gate and go through it, and in that moment you become a child, just as you magically went back in time to these happy, playful younger years.

You see that you stepped into a colorful garden. There are so many different colors here! As you look around, you can see tons of flowers and plants and you can hear many birds singing and also another voice, a soft voice singing a happy song. From behind the tree, a fairy comes out! She has sparkling wings and she's flying towards you with a smile on her face, welcoming you to this fantasy land. Following her are many friendly animals, birds, and butterflies, and you realize that you understand them, you know that they are happy to see you here and they want you to play with them and have a good time. You can pet the rabbit or run around with a dog. There might be a cat rubbing himself against your leg and a butterfly sitting on your arm, gently tickling your skin.

The fairy asks you to follow her and you walk towards the small river that you saw from the top of the hill. There are more fairies there, just playing in the meadow next to the water. Your fairy shows you a few boxes standing on the ground. She tells you that these magical boxes are for worries and sorrows and problems and resentments that you might have brought with you. In this happy land, there's no need for these anymore, so she asks you to put away all the worries and all the problems and all the sorrows and all the resentments into the boxes. And as you put them away, one by one, you feel so much lighter and lighter and you notice peace and happiness filling up your heart and your mind. Once the boxes are full, the fairies close them and take them away high into the sky and you are left with a sense of complete freedom.

Now the fairy shows you to the river - the water in the river is magical. It transforms any negative, sad thoughts into the positive and happy ones. It also heals any pain or illness in your body. All you need to do is to put your hands into the water and wash yourself with it. You can put the water on your face, your arms, your legs, your stomach, and your back, or you can even go into the water and swim in it! And as the water washes away all the things that were not good for you, you feel even more peaceful and happy.

When you're done, you notice that there is a colorful rainbow coming out of the water and there is someone standing next to the rainbow, smiling at you, and waving for you to come closer. As you come up to him, you realize that this is your Guardian Angel! He greets you and gives you a big hug and you can feel unconditional love that is flowing from the Angel's heart into yours. Just feel this love filling up your heart and spreading all around your body and even coming out of it, surrounding you with beautiful light, a light of peace and protection that you can take with you wherever you go.

And as angels can do absolutely anything, your guardian angel wants to take you for a walk up the rainbow. He takes your hand and you start walking up the rainbow. And as you walk, you step on each of the colors of the rainbow and you feel this color filling you up from your feet, all the way up to your head. There is red color ... and orange color ... and yellow color ... and green color ... and blue color ... and purple color and ... white color. You're all the way on top of the rainbow now and what a view it is! You can see a garden below you with the fairies and animals playing by the river. You can see the hill that you walked on as you came to this magical kingdom. And you can see the sky and the clouds that are so close to you that you can even touch them!

Slowly, you're walking down the rainbow with your Guardian Angel. And as you reach the ground, the Angel puts his hand into his pocket and takes out a gift for you! Take the gift into your hands and examine it. What is it? What does it look like? What it is for? Thank your Guardian Angel for this gift and give him a big hug good bye. You know he's always there watching over you, even if you cannot see him.

Now you're about ready to go back home. The fairies surround you and they pick you up and you're flying with them above the garden, all the way back to the lovely entrance gate. Before you step back into the real world, though, the fairies whisper a secret into your ear ... it's something important for you to know. They smile at you and you're smiling back at them. You know that this magical kingdom is just a short walk away and you can always come back here and be a child that you have within - playful, loving and happy. As you step through the gate and become your real age again, you take with you all the love, peace, good feelings.

Once again, you look at the gift that you received from your guardian angel and once again you think of the secret that the fairies told you. And you walk back up the hill, on this lovely natural path, feeling good, feeling happy and peaceful. When you reach the top of the hill, you're ready to come back to here and now, so just take a couple of deep breaths, slowly stretch, open your eyes, and smile!"

"The great man is he who does not lose his child's heart."
~ Mencius ~

Miracle of Manifesting

Paulo Coelho said that an artist can create either from his experience or his imagination. Mirjam was the imagination kind. Her landscapes were filled with unreal colors and her people often showed features of fantasy creatures. She would close her eyes and see dream worlds that have never existed in reality, at least not in our reality. Imagination was an integral part of her being, but she never dreamed of using it in anything else than art.

Mirjam really wanted a car. She loved painting outdoors, far away from the city's disturbing noises and views. But she could only go so far on the bike and there's no way she could carry all her equipment with her. The car would be a salvation. Unfortunately, her savings were empty and she was basically living from pay-check to pay-check. She couldn't see a way to be able to save enough money to buy a car. All she could do was dream about it.

Once, she painted a picture of her dream car. It was highly stained with her imaginary world, of course, but she knew that underneath the rainbows and flowers there was a yellow Volkswagen Beetle. She loved the picture so much that she hung in on her bedroom wall. It added a special kind of atmosphere to her already colorful house.

Mirjam couldn't help but look at the picture often. She passed it so many times during the day and each time a smile came up on her face. Before she went to bed, she stared at it for a long time and as she was falling asleep the image of the car just popped out in front of her eyes. She decided to make it more fun so she pretended that she was sitting behind the wheel of the Beetle driving through peaceful country roads. Sometimes, these scenes even penetrated her dreams! After a night of driving her dream car, she would always feel really happy and excited, just as she was actually driving it in reality!

One evening, Mirjam's friend Kate showed up in her house unexpectedly. They hadn't seen each other since they shared an apartment in college, as Kate moved to another city. They e-mailed often and sometimes talked on the phone, but the river of life took them in different directions. So Mirjam was really surprised to see her dear old friend. They spent all evening talking and it turned out that Kate was in town to collect her inheritance after the death of her eccentric great, great, great aunt. The older lady passed away peacefully at the age of one hundred and one, having a wonderful, interesting life behind her. She loved Kate like a daughter she never had and left her the house and an old Volkswagen Beetle. Kate already had people to move into the house, but was looking to sell the car, as she already owned two of her own and didn't need it.

"That's my dream car!", shouted Mirjam. She got really excited at first, but then remembered "I have not money to buy it, though."

Kate couldn't complain about money - she was an interior designer and had plenty of projects that paid more than she could handle.

"Don't you worry about money, honey" - said Kate, "Just pay me back little by little every month, with no interest, for old times' sake."

Mirjam was so happy that she started jumping around the house like a little girl.

And imagine her surprise when she went to pick up the car the next day and saw that it was a yellow Beetle with rainbows and flowers painted all over it...

"Just as on my picture," she said, "I imagined this car into my life!"

8.

CHOOSE IMAGINATION

"Imagination is everything. It is the preview of life's coming attractions."
~ Albert Einstein ~

Children don't consciously know how important imagination is, but they intuitively use it to create their little worlds. You may not be aware yet, or maybe I mentioned that before, but our minds don't see a difference between what you experience and what you imagine experiencing. Numerous studies and experiments have been performed by scientists on the brain functions and the results shown that in both instances - imagining and experiencing an action, the impulses in the brain were identical. More than that - imagined and experienced situations both created the same emotional responses and even physical sensations and actual permanent changes in the brain! Let me quote one of the experiments that were explained in article in *"Time Magazine"* in the February 2007 issue:

"It was a fairly modest experiment, as these things go, with volunteers trooping into the lab at Harvard Medical School to learn and practice a little five-finger piano exercises. Neuroscientist Alvaro Pascual-Leone instructed the members of one group to play as fluidly as they could, trying to keep to the metronome's 60 beats per minute. Every day for five days, the volunteers practiced for two hours. Then they took a test.

At the end of each day's practice session, they sat beneath a coil of wire that sent a brief magnetic pulse into the motor cortex of their brain, located in a strip running from the crown of the head toward each ear. The so-called transcranial-magnetic-stimulation (TMS) test allows scientists to infer the functions of neurons just beneath the coil. In the piano players, the TMS mapped how much the motor cortex controlled the finger movements needed for the piano exercise. What the scientists found was that after a week of practice the stretch of motor cortex devoted to these finger movements took over surrounding areas like dandelions on a suburban lawn.

The finding was in line with a growing number of discoveries at the time showing that greater use of a particular muscle causes the brain to devote more cortical real estate to it. But Pascual-Leone did not stop there. He extended the experiment by having another group of volunteers merely think about practicing the piano exercise. They played the simple piece of music in their head, holding their hands still while imagining how they would move their fingers. Then they too sat beneath the TMS coil.

When the scientists compared the TMS data on the two groups - those who actually tickled the ivories and those who only imagined doing so - they glimpsed a revolutionary idea about the brain: the ability of mere thought to alter the physical structure and function of our gray matter. For what the TMS revealed was that the region of motor cortex that controls the piano-playing fingers also expanded in volunteers who imagined playing the music - just as it had in those who actually played it."

So what does that mean to you?

First of all, the experiment explains how the thoughts become habits and beliefs on a cellular brain level. When you think a new thought or do an action for a first time, a neural connection is created in the brain. When you repeat that thought or an action, that neural connection strengthens, becomes thicker, and finally the repeated thing becomes embedded into your physical mind and is recognized as true and easy to perform, with time even automatic, just like riding a bike. Have you noticed that once you learn to ride a bike, you will be able to do it even after years of not touching one? The connection in your brain was made and it will stay there for you to use whenever you want to.

Second thing, which I find much more important, is the fact that I mentioned before, that imagining creates the same reaction in the brain as actually experiencing something. So when you imagine riding a bike, the same neural connection is made and strengthened with repetition, as if you were actually riding the bike. Amazing, isn't it? You can learn things by imagining doing them, just as you can change your reality by imagining yourself as a person who is able to achieve your dreams!

THE WORLD IS AS YOU SEE IT

"IKE - The world is what you think it is."
~ First principle of Huna ~

You don't see a world as it is, but as you're conditioned to see it. Your beliefs, habits, your own inner system, built of the neural connections, that you have created in your brain with years and years of practicing your thoughts, will allow you to see and experience only these things that you believe yourself to be able to achieve. In terms of brain functions, your sight is also affected by the neural connections created by the beliefs. The things that you're used to will be easily seen in the surrounding world, while the ideas that are not embedded in your internal map will be very hard to notice.

Do a little test on yourself and write down what you see on the pictures below.

Picture 1

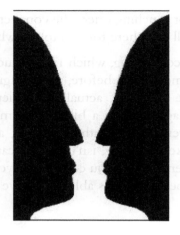

Picture 2

Picture 3

Picture 4

Picture 1 - did you see a man's face or a couple under an arch?
Picture 2 - did you see two faces or a martini glass?
Picture 3 - did you see lady's face or a saxophone player?
Picture 3 - did you see a young woman or an old lady?

If you are like the most people, you probably saw one or the other thing on the pictures. This is because your mind was set to see what's easily visible according to your inner standards and wasn't looking for something else hidden behind what's obvious.

Your viewing of the world around you works just the same. You only see what you think about. Have you noticed that if you think about having a child, there are suddenly pregnant women or mothers with babies everywhere? Or you dream of that red Audi and all of the sudden that car is on all the roads and parking lots! Has it been there all along or did it magically multiply just because you want to have it? Of course, the cars, pregnant women, and babies exist in the same quantities as before you started thinking about them, but you haven't noticed them before because they were out of your range of thoughts.

Just as you don't see things that you don't think about, you don't see opportunities and possibilities that don't fit your inner belief system. If you don't believe you will be able to fulfill the obligations of a managerial job, you don't see the positions advertised in the daily paper, because your mind won't allow you to. And even if you do happen to notice it, you don't see the skills required to get the position in yourself! If you believe you don't deserve to be in a fulfilling relationship, you only date men who don't treat you right, simply because you don't notice anyone else around you, even if a nice, kind man tries to start the conversation. If you think you're fat and ugly, you only buy chips and fast food when you're out and salads magically disappear from the restaurant menu!

The process of becoming aware will help you realize your inner belief system and broaden your view of reality and its possibilities. But you can help yourself to change your inner vision by using imagination.

⁓෴⁓

THE LAW OF ATTRACTION

The above paragraphs explain the way imagination works on the physical body-brain level. But there's another aspect of this subject that has just as much importance.

Many books were written about the Law of Attraction, Esther and Jerry Hick's *Ask and it is Given* being one of the easier ones to understand, so I will not dig too deep into the subject, but only cover the main points, leaving the curious reader to find more details in other publications.

The Law of Attraction Quantum Physics states that *"Thoughts become things"*. It works on the principle that everything in the world is energy, as Einstein once said. Quantum physicists found that there are smaller particles than electrons that the whole world is constructed with. Those particles – quantums – are not solid, as we previously thought of electrons – they are forms of vibrating energy. So the matter is actually not solid, but a billions and trillions of tiny vibrating particles of energy. Similarly, a thought is also energy, in a form of wave of these tiny particles, sent into the universe. So if thoughts are energy and matter is energy, then our thoughts can attract material things into our lives, according to most important rule of the Law of Attraction: *"Like attracts like."*

Just think of all the times that you thought about someone intensively and the person called you? Or dreaming deeply about something, only to have strange coincidences bring you this desired thing? Well, you may ask: *"What about all the times I wanted something and it didn't happen?"*

The Law of Attraction has its rules that you will need to follow.

Now think of imagination again in the context of creating such vibrational frequency that will attract things that you want into your life. You need to create specific thoughts and feel your desires in your mind and heart, but it can be hard to be positive and open to those good new things if all you see in the world around you are pain, negativity, and other things that you don't want to experience anymore. That's where imagination comes in. By creating positive visions in your mind, you will bring yourself up to the level of vibration that will bring these visions into your life.

IMAGINE THE IMPOSSIBLE

"The only things that stand between a person and what they want in life are the will to try it and the faith to believe it's possible."
~ Richard M. De Vos ~

Because the brain sees what you imagine just as it does reality, and the Law of Attraction responds to your vibrational call created by your thoughts, you can imagine your way to happiness. It may be hard to pretend in reality that your life is positive and good if you feel sick or unhappy. But imagination has no limits! That's why it makes *choice* and *change* so much easier!

Imagining is like creating a full color, surround sound, 3D movie in your mind. Your visions need to be clear and precise, though, and first of all, filled with positive, happy images of what you want to be, do, or have. Before giving you a visualization exercise, I want to make you aware of few rules that will either make or break your imagined future.

❧❦❧

7 RULES OF IMAGINATION

1. *Imagine Positive.* Think of what you want to be, do, or have, not of what you *don't* want. For some reason, your subconscious mind doesn't hear the word *"no"*. It only creates a vision of the thing you're concentrating on. So if you concentrate on health, you will see and attract more health. If you concentrate on not wanting to be sick, you actually create more sickness! Therefore, before creating your visualization, write down what it is that you DO want in a positive, clear statement and then build your imaginary scenes around it.

2. *Imagine in the Now.* If you think of wanting something, you put yourself in a state of wanting, not achieving it. Your brain creates a thought of wanting and embeds it into your brain, summoning the "wanting" vibrations instead of the "achieving" ones. Same with saying that you *will* have it someday. You move your desired outcome into a never ending future where it will stay forever. It is the main principle of the affirmations to say them in a present tense and it actually creates a barrier for some people that they cannot cross. *"Isn't saying I'm rich a lie? I cannot lie to myself."* If you look at it from mainly physical, material perspective that yes, it would be a lie. But we're not working on a physical level here. Just think of the way children pretend-play. They are actors putting all of themselves into their roles. And that creates happy, positive, good feelings, feelings that summon the energy, feelings that make you believe that it is possible to be rich, thin or loved. And that's the point of putting your visions in a present tense. Once you believe it - you will achieve it!

3. *Imagine Yourself.* Make sure to put YOU in your visions! Put yourself in the center of the scenes, be the main character of the imagined story. Add details to it and make it more real, more believable. Even better if you can see the imagined scenes through your own eyes! If you think of that car that you want to have, you only open your vision to seeing the car all around you. But what if you imagine sitting behind the wheel, actually driving it, and seeing the landscape that you pass on your way? That's where you want to be - in the car, not next to it.

4. *Imagine the Feeling.* Make your visions as colorful and full of life as possible, so they can create good feelings in your heart. Feelings of already having achieved your dream - the excitement, the happiness, the pride, the joy. Feelings strengthen the thoughts that you think, make them more believable to you, and more possible to achieve. And feelings are the driving power of the Law of Attraction. With more power, you raise your vibration higher, faster, and easier.

5. *Imagine the End Result.* Often, people think they need to have it all figured out from the start. Trying to find ways to make things happen creates tension, worry, and stress. These are not positive feelings that will give you motivation and strength to reach your dreams or goals. They can easily stop you in your tracks, making your believe you are not good/smart/strong enough to do it, or that it's so hard that it's actually impossible. That's it. Your dream is finished and your life stays as it is. One needs to have a little faith in the Universe, God, Angels, the Creator, or whatever Higher Power you believe in. You don't think this whole beautiful, magical, complex world was created by humans? Just look around you at the beauty Earth that you walk on, the amazing way the Universe works to support all life processes, even those in your own body. If you were given a power to sustain your body in this material reality, why can't you believe that you will also be given help to make your life journey

happy and fulfilling? Have faith that if you want something bad enough and it will make you happy and enrich the life of those around you, you will find ways to make it happen. The Universe will help you. So imagine yourself at the end of the road, joyful and happy as you hold hands with this special someone, sitting on a swing of your dream house, watching your children play as the sun goes down ... Now that's a happy vision, isn't it?

6. ***Don't limit your possibilities.*** What I will say now may sound contradicting to what I said before about being precise in your visions, but when you read further you will see that actually it's not. You do need to have clear idea of what you want from life, what you will choose your life to be like. Be precise about the *qualities* of what you want, but don't limit your possibilities with stubbornly saying that you want only this exact thing or nothing else! I have mentioned before about choosing wisely. If you choose this one particular person you want to spend your life with, it may not happen, as this person also has free will and his or her heart may belong to someone else already. What if you don't really know this person, you only look at him through your "belief-system" glasses and in reality he's not someone you will be happy with? With enough strong will you may end up with him but as the illusions melt away you will realize that this relationship it not what you were dreaming of. That's why it's better to create a list of qualities you want in your partner, job or house. That way you give the Universe free hand to bring you the things you *really* want, not just these you feel you need when you're still locked in your world of learned beliefs and habits. And in time you will see more of such people and opportunities that can make you truly happy.

7. ***Don't overdo it.*** I have noticed when I practice yoga that the more I push myself into going deeper into a position, the harder it becomes to reach my desired angle. So I tried not to push it, but to let it go. As I let my breath guide me in releasing tensions,

I am able to achieve much more than through the act of force. I am even able to go past the limits I thought my physical body had! It's the same with any goal or dream. The more you force it, the harder it becomes to reach it. Mike Dooley in his book *Infinite Possibilities* recommends visualizing your goal for four minutes a day and I strongly agree with him, based on my own experiences. Four minutes is enough to light the fire of good happy feelings in your heart, to create positive strong thoughts in your mind, and to raise yourself to the higher level of vibration. That's your part. Let the Universe handle the rest!

"The real power does not come from the force but from the gentle art of letting go"
~ Lorelai I. Dali ~

IMAGINING YOUR FUTURE

Are you ready to start working on creating the future of your dreams? Start by asking yourself a question:

What if there were no limits to what I can be, do, or have? What would I choose?

Because the choice *is* yours. You have started this journey already when you picked up this book. But what do you really want and how to achieve it with the help of imagination?

I created a Goal Spreadsheet for you to specify what it is that you want in life (find in Appendix section at the end of the book). Start with the smaller goal or dream and take time to fill out the form honestly and according to the Seven Rules of Imagination. Once you achieve the smaller goal, it will be easier to work on something bigger. Don't start with the hardest ones to avoid disappointments. Remember that imagining your way to happiness is a skill just like driving a car. Let yourself develop this skill on easier roads before you move onto the highways!

There is a possibility that you may find a resistance or blockage that will stand on your way to reaching your goal. It may come from negative attitudes or feelings towards yourself or the way the world works. Or low self-esteem and fear. I gave you a great tool in Chapter 5 - *The STOP Technique*, which will help you transform these thoughts, beliefs, and feelings. I have also included a releasing technique in *Manifesting Change Meditation* below to let go of any blockage on the energy level.

~◌❀◌❀◌~

MANIFESTING CHANGE MEDITATION

Part 1 - Release

* Start by creating the state of mind and body relaxation.
* State your goal in a positive way in your mind or out loud (based on your Goal Spreadsheet)
* Ask yourself - is there anything blocking me from achieving this goal? See it as a picture or a symbol in your inner mind.
* Once you see the cause of the resistance, let it dissolve in front of your eyes. You can let is shrink until it's gone, or make it more and more blurry until it disappears or let it melt down until it's no more. If you have problems letting this go, imagine the golden light shining down on it from above, turning it into gold light itself, until the picture is gone.

Part 2 - Achieve

* Take a few deep breaths, breathing in through your head, taking the air from above, and letting it out through your feet, letting it go into the earth.

* Imagine yourself as if your dream has already manifested. See all the details, hear all the sounds, smell and taste, if necessary, add props and people to the scene, and make sure to put yourself in it! Add colors and good feelings. Smile inside and out.
* Think about your dream again, create a small picture of it, and hold this picture in your hands.
* Put your hands onto your heart and feel the good, positive feelings of your dream already happening! It can be happiness, excitement, pride, freedom, love or anything else that makes you feel good.
* Look up towards heavens and send your dream from your hands to the Universe to let it manifest.

Practice your visualization once a day for four minutes. When you feel that nothing stops you from reaching your dream anymore, you can omit the first part and just concentrate on imagining the future. I recommend working on each goal for at least twenty-one days, up to ninety days. You will see changes take place and know when it's time to move on to something else.

❧❦❧❦❧

SPECIAL AIDS

You can help yourself imagining your end result with more physical props. There are two things that I found working like magic.

VISION BOARD

A *Vision Board* (also called a Treasure Map, a Dream Board or Creativity Collage) is typically a poster board on which you paste or collage images that you've torn out from various magazines or printed from the web.

When you surround yourself with images of who you want to become, what you want to have, where you want to live, or where you want to go on holidays, your life changes to match those images and those desires. You tell the Universe - this is what I want! *And* you have it put down on paper! Then the Law of Attraction starts to draw things from your board into your life.

A vision board adds clarity to your desires and feeling to your visions. It's an irreplaceable help to your visualizations of the future and a powerful tool you can use daily.

To create a *Vision Board*, you need a stack of old magazines with pictures. As you look through them, cut out the ones that appeal to you - they can be the things that you want to have or be or symbols that mean something that you desire. Or just things that make you feel good and happy. Alternatively to the magazines, you can take some time to search the internet for pictures symbolizing your dreams, then print them out in full color. You will also need a happy picture or a few of yourself to place right in the middle of your collage. Or to glue over a face of someone wearing that wedding dress that you dream about!

Once you have your pictures, lay them out on your poster board and look at them again. Toss away the ones that don't fit your vision anymore and place the others around the poster. You can add the power of Feng Shui, by placing images in appropriate areas of Ba-Gua Square (see Appendix)!

You can add words or color things onto the board too. Use your creativity as you like. And don't worry about the quality of your drawings - the board must appeal to you and you only!

Place the board in a visible place, if possible, and look at it daily. As you look at the pictures, imagine the scene of your dream already happening and add feelings to it. If you live with others and want to keep the vision board for your eyes only, take it out every day and let the imagination do its work!

ACTING "AS IF"

Again we go back to childhood years. Acting "as if" is a game of pretending that you already live the life that you desire. Just like child moves furniture around to build a castle, so you can change your surroundings and do little actions that will prepare you for this new exciting change to come into your life. You ready yourself in your mind for these new things so when they do come you will easily accept them as your new reality.

Just think of pregnant women preparing the room for the child's arrival. She will buy the right furniture, paint the walls, get clothes for the baby, and sit on the rocking chair imagining what it will be like sitting there with baby in her arms. The baby is not here yet, but she knows it will be here soon so she needs to be ready.

It's the same with anything else that you want in life. If you want to have a new car, why not clear out a garage and buy a new key ring with the car's logo? If you want to share a life with perfect partner, why not make a space in your closet for his things and put two settings on the table even if you eat dinner alone?

It sounds silly, I know. You're a serious grown-up, adult person. What will people say if you start acting so childish? You don't need to show off what you're doing to the whole wide world, as long as you know that you're preparing for something new to come and acting "as if" makes it fun to wait!

"A rock pile ceases to be a rock pile the moment a single man contemplates it, bearing within him the image of a cathedral."
~ Antoine de Saint - Exupery ~

Miracle of Letting Go

It was about a year after Mirjam started counseling that was to help her with her anxiety. She really liked her therapist and already saw improvements in the way she handled stress. Her confidence level was much higher than before and she was learning to love and accept herself. But it was a hard process. She remembered many situations that she made herself forget in the past, as they hurt too much. Now she had to face them and understand how they affected the ways she deals with life now. She became aware of how her parents' inability to show love made her believe that she didn't deserve to be happy. She reviewed her past relationships and recognized that she allowed people to treat her badly and without respect. She realized that she was used by her friends and had no real support system when growing up. These were tough memories to deal with, especially that they still held her heart in their iron claws.

At first, Mirjam didn't understand how people could treat her so unfairly. She was deeply hurt by their selfishness and ignorance. She felt like a victim and only her pillow knew how much sorrow was in her heart. She played situations over and over in her head and felt the soul-breaking pain each time.

After a while, she realized that going over the past will not change it and she's just causing herself more unhappiness reliving it every day. She was now willing to see it from another point of view. She tried to put herself in their shoes and understood that her parents, her friends, her lovers had their own view of the world, very different than hers. Often, they hadn't even realized that they'd hurt her, blinded by their own beliefs, habits, and inner barriers. That understanding gave her mental peace, but her heart still ached.

Mirjam knew she needed to forgive her perpetrators and let the past go. But this was something she didn't know how to do. Wouldn't forgiving mean that she agreed with what they did? Wouldn't it mean that she deserved all that pain? She was confused.

The answer came to her in the form of a stranger. She was sitting in the park when an older man, reminding her of her grandfather, asked if he could join her. She was in a bad mood, but felt it was be rude to refuse, so she nodded. And so he sat next to her on a bench. He said it was a lovely day and that he was very happy to be in the park today. Mirjam tried to be nice, but she was lost in her thoughts about the past so her confirming "Yes, it is," sounded really fake.

"What is wrong, child?" the man asked.

Mirjam wanted to pretend everything was fine, but for some strange reason the truth came out of her mouth.

"I'm just sad because I'm broken," she said. "I've been treated badly all my life and even though I try to forget the past, I'm still hurting. I will never be able to be happy."

The man took her hand into his hand and said: "If you've never seen the darkness, you will not know the light, even if it shines straight into your face. But it's up to you to let go of the darkness once it has fulfilled its purpose, so that you can see the light everywhere."

Then he went on to talk about how happy he was that he was able to walk to the park today, as his friend is lying sick in bed and cannot enjoy this lovely weather. He took out two apples, giving her one and saying how glad he is that he found the real kind, not those plastic ones they sell in the supermarkets now. These "real ones" taste just like the apples from his childhood. He smiled and told her how pretty her hair was and that he's jealous because he's left with none. But he pointed at his hat and said that he's really thankful for his hat, as people usually look onto his shiny bald head in hope to see their future. Then he burst out with such a contagious laughter that Mirjam could not help but laugh with him.

The old man left soon, but Mirjam looked at the world around her differently. She now saw the blooming flowers and the ducks swimming on the pond. Children were running around playing with their dog. The apple really tasted amazing. She didn't have to go anywhere, but could just sit here and enjoy this lovely day.

Then she felt grateful for this day and the chance to be able to enjoy it. No matter the past, she cannot change it, can she? But she can decide not to let the past affect her present. She realized how happy she was to be able to be alive and make choices that will create her happy future.

9.

CHOOSE GRATITUDE

"You cannot build a happy future on the foundations of unhappy present."
~ Lorelai I. Dali ~

Would you be reading this book if you were totally and utterly happy and fulfilled? Probably not.

It's great that you're looking for solutions and ways to improve your life in the future. But you must realize that the future is something you will never reach, as when it happens, it becomes your today. So why move your life into some indefinite time and space and not start living it right now?

SHORT WORD ON THE PAST

The past is gone and you cannot change it. It is important, as your experiences in the past led you to where you are today. That's true, that things happened in the past. Some of them were very powerful and traumatic and made you feel like you're not in control or that you don't matter. We've all experienced hurt, pain, disappointments, and sadness in the past, but does it mean that we need to hold on to these feelings and relieve the unhappy experiences over and over? You can treat them as learning experiences that they were, understand your lessons, and move on with new knowledge that can benefit you in the future. You cannot change the past, but you can change how it affects you in the present. You can either dwell on what you've been through and drag it with you wherever and *whenever* you go, or you can let it go.

Do you want your past to run your life or can you take control of your life into your own hands? It's *your* choice.

> *"One day at a time - this is enough. Do not look back and grieve over the past, for it is gone: and do not be troubled about the future, for it has not yet come. Live in the present, and make it so beautiful that it will be worth remembering."*
> ~ Ida Scott Taylor ~

LIFE IS A LEARNING EXPERIENCE

Would you really want to have only happy experiences all the time? Just think about it. If you've never seen darkness, would you appreciate the light? If you've never experienced anything bad, you wouldn't realize when something good happens, simply because you wouldn't have anything to compare it to.

People who had it easy in life are actually some of the unhappiest people on earth. They never had to work for anything, so they don't appreciate all the good things they have. They haven't had a chance to learn from their experiences and so they haven't grown as humans and they were not able to develop deeper compassion, empathy, and awareness. Their lives may seem happy on the outside, but in fact they are empty and shallow, lacking the most important part of human experience - the learning journey. Why would you want that?

On the other hand, some of the most amazing people I met have been through what you could call "hell." There were abused, mistreated, taken advantage of, unappreciated, and had to walk uphill most of the time. But these tough experiences made them realize their inner power and appreciate the simpler things in life, like a kind word, gentle smile, love of their family and friends, and the joy of helping others. They found deeper meaning of life through their tough lessons. And they learned to *deal* with life's ups and downs in constructive ways.

I don't advocate that you can only learn through suffering. You are meant to be happy. But life is just like a wave. It is a road made out of ups and downs, hills and valleys, days and nights. The wave patterns are all around us. The sound is a wave. The light is a wave. The quantums are waves. And the thoughts are waves. Why would the flow of life be any different? There are better days and worse days and your role is to understand this nature of life and allow it to happen while choosing not to let it affect how you feel. You cannot control the weather, but you can choose whether it will affect you. That is the biggest power you have, the power to choose how you feel about what happens.

"My policy is to learn from the past, focus on the present, and dream about the future. I'm a firm believer in learning from adversity. Often the worst of times can turn to your advantage. My life is a study of that."
~ Donald Trump ~

LIFE IS HARD?

The level of difficulty of a task does not depend on how hard the task is, but on your attitude towards it. There are people who work in the mines and enjoy it. You would think it's pretty hard to dig into the earth in cold and darkness, wouldn't you? If you view something as hard, it will be hard for you and will drag on forever. In the same time your friend may do the same thing faster with a smile on his face. The difference is your attitudes. If you approach something with a preconceived idea about it, the idea will make it happen so. You make your life happen, remember? Your thoughts do create your reality. If you choose to look at something as hard, it will be hard. If you think it's bearable or even fun, it will be so much easier for you! Why not take life as a fun journey and get excited about the challenges that come your way? Try it for a day and see the difference your attitude makes!

There is a very thin line between anxiety and excitement. Bodily signals are actually the same for both!

I remember a famous musician talking to a reporter before the show. The reporter asked if he ever felt stage fright. The musician said: *"No, I don't. When I stand backstage right before the show I feel my heart pounding, I breathe faster, my hands start to shake a bit and I have butterflies in my stomach. That's how excited I get!"* Heart pounding, faster breathing, shaking hands, butterflies, maybe even dizziness, ... That sounds just like an anxiety attack, doesn't it? The symptoms of excitement and anxiety are the same, and the difference in the experience is how you look at it! Do you choose anxiety or excitement? Fear or joy? I get nervous before every class that I teach and every client that I meet. When I realize my feelings though, I stop, throw my hands in the air, and shout out loud: *"I am sooo excited to be able to do that! Thank you, thank you, thank you!"*

What if you experience something that really stops you in your tracks and you just can't get enough inner power to get up and deal with it? You're human, and it's ok to have moments like that too. The fourth principle of Toltec knowledge written down by Don Miguel Ruiz in his amazing book *Four Agreements* says:

"Always Do Your Best. Your best is going to change from moment to moment; it will be different when you are healthy as opposed to sick. Under any circumstance, simply do your best and you will avoid self-judgment, self-abuse, and regret."

Don't be too hard on yourself and just be human, imperfect but divine in his imperfections. And if your "best" means that you just cannot deal with a situation in a strong, constructive way, just remember another important fact of life: *change is inevitable.* Life flows like a wave and won't stop. Whatever you are going through will pass. And it can be a great comfort to know that in tough moments. You are not stuck in them. Any situation, any circumstance, any experience will pass. At some point on the road, you will see a turning sign directing you towards the better days. Just remember that *you* are the driver and it's up to you to take that exit!

Sometimes, people hold on to things, whether good or bad, pretending not to see the change happening. It's understandable if you're going through happy moments - you want them to last forever. But you cannot hold on to them indefinitely and such resistance creates circumstances that will force the change upon you, sometimes in a really unpleasant manner. You cannot change the ways of nature. There is no point trying to stand still in the flowing river. If you allow the flow to take you, you will be amazed at what is waiting for you after that turn you can barely see now! Why not be excited about it already?

It can also be helpful to *believe.* The Universe supports you. You are here not by some strange random act, but for a purpose. And your purpose is to follow your own special path, "your legend", just like Paulo Coelho's *Alchemist.* And to be happy along the way. Allow that amazing Higher Power to help you. Believe that there is always a way out and you will be shown the way.

❦

THE PATH OF GRATITUDE

"All of us tend to put off living. We are all dreaming of some magical rose garden over the horizon - instead of enjoying the roses that are blooming outside our windows today."
~ Dale Carnegie ~

What is gratitude? It's not just being thankful for what you have. It's enjoying the moment. It's the art of being present in the Now.

It's good to have dreams and goals. The sailor needs to know his destination port in order to catch the right winds. Dream, plan, set goals, and imagine them happening. Strive to be the best you can be and reach your highest potential. Learn, read, attend workshops and classes that will bring you closer to what you want your life to be someday. But don't let dreaming about the future rob you of the beauty of today!

We already have so much! But isn't this common to appreciate what we had only after it's gone? Don't make that mistake. Start practicing gratitude right now, from this moment. Make a conscious decision to enjoy your life in every moment, as each moment brings things for you to enjoy.

You might say: *"But I'm sick and broke and my partner just left me. I don't have anything to enjoy in life."* Is this true really? You are alive. You have air to breathe and amazing body that works in mysterious ways to keep itself going, despite environmental pollution, unhealthy food-like products, and overly stressful lifestyle that you put it through. You most probably have a roof over your head and food to eat, which is more that many people on the planet have. You have friends, family, or at least a dog that cares about you, or maybe flowers that need your attention. Everyone can find at least one living creature that needs them. You have clean water to drink, transportation in case you need to go from one place to another, medication for when you get sick, and so many other inventions that make your life easier. Look around the Earth and see the beauty that this magnificent planet creates for you to enjoy day after day, even though it's being beaten and mistreated by the human species enormously. And if you cannot relate to any of the above - you have your eyes that allow you to read this book right now! As long as you are alive you can choose how you will direct the rest of the movie called *"My Life"*.

Wallowing in sadness never helped anyone feel better. Complaining doesn't make a difference. Gratitude does. Look around you now at your surroundings, in your inner world, think about your work, relationships, hobbies, and write down ten things that you are happy you have in your life. Things you can appreciate or maybe those that you would miss if there were gone?

I bought my daughter a small notebook and asked her to write down on the first page *"My Gratitude Diary"*. Every evening, she reviews her day and writes down things she's thankful for that day. As she does, she remembers these special situations and she's happy about them once again. The gift of appreciation and gratitude is one of the fundamental lessons you can teach your children. If they can see the magnificence of their daily lives, they will never have feelings of lack, the feelings that awaken need to have more and more, to build material structures around ourselves that will serve as illusions of happiness.

We have all we need to be happy. We can add more things to make our life experience more interesting if we want to. But not because we feel we have to, as we won't be happy without them.

Find your inner happiness first by practicing gratitude in the now and build your even better future on these foundations.

Complaining is the opposite of gratitude and it's something that we need to unlearn as fast as possible. By complaining, you focus your attention on what you *don't* want. And therefore you make it stronger. The more you complain, the more reasons you will have to complain about. The more you thank, the more things you will have to be thankful for. Would you rather have things to complain about or to be thankful for?

It is not to say that if you have a problem, you cannot talk about it or should pretend that it doesn't exist. Talking about your problem while focusing on finding a solution, is a positive and constructive process. But dwelling on a problem is not. If you can fix whatever bothers you, do it now. But if you can't, why focus your attention on it? Instead, look around and notice the positive things that surround you. Maybe the sun is shining really nicely today. Or you just had a very tasty breakfast with your partner. See the things that make you happy and *shift* you attention to them. And when someone asks you how your day went, start with the good things first, leaving the bad for later. After you're done talking about the situations you enjoyed, you may even forget to mention these little difficulties that happened along the way!

And remember the Law of Attraction? It does state that whatever you focus on you attract into your life. If you focus on the negative situations, you're attracting more negative situations. Do you really want that? Stop complaining, whining, and dwelling on the problems. Choose the happy path in life - the Path of Gratitude and notice how your life experiences will change along with your attitude.

༄༅࿐࿐

FORGIVENESS

Many of us face situations in life that are hard to understand. People live in poverty, violence, and abuse. There are crimes, wars, and injustice. If you have experienced such dramatic circumstances, it's hard to believe in the deeper meaning or recall gratitude in such chaos and tragedy. But you realize by now that staying in the state of being a victim does not solve anything and keeps you exactly where you don't want to be. In order to break away from the vicious circle of reliving your past and recreating the same future over and over, you must turn to forgiveness.

We understand forgiveness as letting go of the pain and hurt, while still remembering that it happened. It can prove to be a very difficult task. If you think that someone hurt you, the feelings of being victimized, offended, mistreated keeps lingering for a very long time. Even if you intellectually explain the situation and understand the motives or problems that led someone to treat you in such way, the feelings remain and keep poisoning you from the inside. Yes, the unforgiveness hurts *you*, not the person who mistreated you! They probably forgot about it a long time ago, if they even noticed how their behavior or words affected you. But you carry this burden with you every day of your life!

That reminds me of an old Buddhist story:

"Two Buddhist Monks were on a journey, one was a senior monk, the other a junior monk. During their journey they approached a raging river and on the river bank stood a young lady. She was clearly concerned about how she would get to the other side of the river without drowning.

The junior monk walked straight past her without giving it a thought and he crossed the river. The senior monk picked up the woman and carried her across the river. He placed her down, they parted ways with woman and on they went with the journey.

As the journey went on, the senior monk could see some concern on the junior monk's mind, he asked what was wrong. The junior monk replied: 'How could you carry her like that? You know we can't touch women, it's against our way of life'. The senior monk answered, 'I left the woman at the river's edge a long way back, why are you still carrying her?' "

Do you really want to carry your pain with you all your life? ...

I would like to introduce you to another approach to letting go called "Radical Forgiveness", created by Collin C. Tipping. Tipping looks at the act of forgiveness from a spiritual point of view without judgment of right and wrong. From a higher perspective, everything happens to us for a reason. Before we come to this material world, we create a kind of plan of what we want to experience and learn. Sometimes we can only learn though hardship and pain and so individual souls from our soul family agree to play different roles in our life journey, in order for us to experience desired situations. And each and every one of these situation brings us closer to finding our own divinity and the path of Love. So if we set it all up ourselves beforehand, is any situation that we experience really good or bad? Or are they just parts of our necessary journey? And if there is nothing wrong that happened, even though it was painful to experience particular situation, there is really nothing to forgive, is there? How's that for an insight!

Please read Tipping's book for more details about Radical Forgiveness, as this is an amazing transformational tool that can give you much needed inner peace.

If we allow ourselves to shift to a different approach to life's difficulties, viewing them all as lessons, grateful for all we have and always looking for things that make us happy, we can then keep on easily flowing in the river of experiences, growing at a deep soul level and able to enjoy things even during the hardest of times.

⇛❉❉❉⇚

"There is no such thing as the 'opposite' of Love. Love is the only energy in our reality that has no opposite - although there are many expressions of Love that look like its opposite. Only a Master can see they are all the same...and thus, only a Master can forgive that which is done in the name of Fear."
~ Neale Donald Walsch ~

Miracle of Caring

Mirjam remembers the days when she wasn't aware. She would eat her lunch at fast food restaurants, go home after work with a sub, and watch television until late, feeling bloated and groggy. Exercising? "I'm too tired." Home cooked meal? "Sorry, no time." Meditation? "Too boring." When she felt sick, she would go to the doctor who prescribed some pills and she thought she felt better for a short while. She didn't take care of herself because she was too busy taking care of others or building illusions of happiness.

"I wish I knew before," - Mirjam thought.

She learned that to be able to take care of others, she needed to take care of herself first. She started educating herself and as her awareness grew, she started feeling ashamed at how she treated her body, mind, and soul. She was poisoning herself slowly and was surprised why she didn't have energy to do things. She didn't take time to relax and her stress level grew to the point that she was about to lose her mind. She didn't look beyond the material world and felt alone and hopeless.

But Mirjam was still young, so it was not all lost yet. She thanked herself for not giving in to Rob, one of her exes. He thought drugs and alcohol were the answers to all life's problems. "Your parents pissed you off? Have a puff, you won't care about it anymore," he used to say, handing her a joint. "You're sad? Have a drink, it will make you feel better in no time." She did have a drink here or there, but she always controlled herself. But Rob? She saw him a few months ago, again. She remembered him as this funny talkative guy with sparkling blue eyes. Mirjam hardly recognized the skinny man calling after her on the street. His face was of some kind of grayish color, with dark circles under his eyes. When he spoke, words came out weirdly slow and it took him about five minutes to finish a sentence. Later, she read that drugs irreversibly destroy brain cells. She saw with her own eyes what it meant.

Mirjam was choosing smart now. She was committed to educate herself in well-being issues and to spread the knowledge to her family and friends. Sometimes, she would give herself a break with an occasional ice-cream or day off from exercise, but she now really felt the difference in how her body and mind worked if taken care of. This was priceless.

10.

CHOOSE RESPONSIBLY

It's an amazing journey to evolve from being a caterpillar into a butterfly. Just like that tiny worm-like insect, you were unaware of your true inner potential to become someone spectacular. To be able to fly high in the sky and reach your innermost dreams was not something you ever thought possible. But here you are, conscious of that deep inner strength that comes from your free will to choose what your life would be like, to make decisions of what you think, what you say, and what you feel, to choose actions that will benefit you based on your desires, not on unconscious programs that used to run your life. You're aware of the potential you can reach and you have tools that will get you there. Now that's powerful, isn't it?

You make your choices, so do make them consciously and get informed about possible consequences of your decisions. When you take your life into your own hands, you become responsible for your future so be mindful to choose only what is the best for you.

Thanks to the power of the thoughts that you choose, you can create your reality. With that comes a responsibility to make this reality a good one, not just for you but for those around you too. Each of us creates a separate world with his beliefs, and that world overlaps the worlds of those that we interact with: our parents, children, lovers, friends, bosses, employees, clients, and co-workers. Together these small worlds create societies, cultures, countries, and religions. And each of your private worlds is a part of those bigger groups, affecting how they work, making a difference. They all affect the Earth and our solar system and even the whole universe.

What you do, you don't do in silence. Every action has a reaction. Your actions affect other people and your planet. Therefore, it is important to be very conscious of what you do, say, feel, and think.

❧❦❧

RESPONSIBILITY FOR YOURSELF

Do you know that sometimes what you want is not what you actually need? If you work on your awareness, with time you will notice things that you do on an autopilot, things that you learned to like. Take eating sweets for example. Humans, just like other mammals, are not built to eat tons of sugar. You were given sweets as a child and learned to like it, use it excessively and soon it became automatic, physical addiction to the substance. Now you just eat it out of habit.

Educate yourself about a healthy lifestyle, make decisions to choose nourishment instead of stomach fillers, exercise instead of watching television, and meditate instead of going out for drinks. You will thank yourself when you're older and surrounded with people who look twenty years older than they actually are, suffering from digestion, breathing, and emotional problems, because they didn't take care of themselves when they had a chance.

Be aware of your limits and learn to ask for help. There are times when you may not be able to do things physically or some knowledge may be out of your area of expertise or talents. People are different for a reason, so don't try to do every single thing yourself, but find others who can help you in tasks that are not your strongest points. That way you will have more time and energy to use those special talents of yours for your and other's benefit.

Remember to take care of your mental and emotional health and if you need to use help of others, don't think yourself weak. You may be great at helping or giving advice to others, but when it comes to you, it's natural that you may need assistance of someone else. We don't see ourselves objectively and that's why it's helpful to ask for advice or support from friends or health professionals, whether western or alternative. Taking time to wind down and relax or getting help in this relaxation is not a sign of weakness but wisdom, as if you don't take care of yourself you will not be able to share your special gifts with others.

Last but not least, when making career, education, or relationship choices, think of what can bring you closer to your divine purpose, not what can satisfy a temporary lack. Look at the bigger picture and give yourself more time to get where you want to be. Don't settle for less. You deserve to be happy in the deepest sense of this word, not just now, but forever.

Making choices comes in pair with taking responsibility for the outcomes and as scary as it may seem to some people, it's the only way to have the kind of life that you dream of.

"A man may fail many times but he isn't a failure until he begins to blame somebody else."
~ J. Paul Getty ~

❧⊚❦❦⊚❧

RESPONSIBILITY FOR OTHERS

First thing to know is that you are not responsible for other people's reactions. So don't blame yourself if people misinterpret your intentions, if you made them clear. Don't feel ashamed for your parent's or friends' behavior, as it has nothing to do with you. You cannot hold yourself responsible for what is not yours. But you are responsible for *your* actions and need to be aware that they affect others, not just you.

If you are driven by Love (see chapter 2), then I don't need to remind you of the importance of thinking with your heart. But even the best of people can sometimes forget that the tools that they have in their hands can be used as very powerful weapons if handled without consideration. We are all human and deserve to be treated with respect, compassion, and understanding. We were all born and each of us will die when the time comes. It doesn't matter where you come from, what is your skin color, or your education when it comes to our basic needs to have food, shelter, and love. Each of us can experience sickness, sadness, and hardship, as well as happiness, love, and fulfillment. It's not up to you to judge another, as you have no idea what brought him to be or act the way he does. He will reap what he sowed, this is the way nature works, so don't try to force the punishment on anyone, whether by actions or harsh words.

Be mindful of the words that come out of your mouth. Words can hurt just like actions do and such wounds may be very hard to heal. You have been conditioned to learn certain behaviors and beliefs though what your parents and teachers told you. So you realize how much the words can affect a person, even if said without any particular purpose. What if your words touch a soft spot in another's heart? What if you confirm their inner fears?

Words that fall on fertile ground grow roots in the mind. Make sure that you think before you speak and be clear and considerate in what you want to express.

It's the same with actions. Just as you look twice before crossing the street, think twice before doing anything that may affect others. Treat people like you would like to be treated and you will not make a mistake of hurting anyone's feelings, well-being, or security. Be especially mindful around children, as they learn more from example than by explanation. If you want your child to help others, help those in need yourself. If you want to have a tidy house, start with cleaning your own bedroom and make sure your child sees that. If you want them to eat healthy, eat fruits and vegetables yourself. You can show them what can be done by doing it.

Your example can help adults around you, as well. If you consistently work on self-improvement, being positive, and creating the world of your dreams, others will see your successes and start asking about your secrets. By showing them the tools that work for you, you can make a huge difference in their lives. Such difference cannot be done by simply talking the talk. Walking the walk has much more teaching potential. It's especially important if you are in a therapeutic work field yourself. By telling stories of your struggles and triumphs, you can show your client that you are human just like they are and had your difficulties, but were able to overcome them. If you could, why couldn't they?

Use your power of choice for the good of others, while remembering to choose yourself first.

❦

RESPONSIBILITY FOR THE PLANET

It saddens me deeply to see how people treat the planet they live on, as if it was just some temporary stop on their road that they will never go back to again, so who cares if they leave it dirty and destroyed? As if we didn't need it to survive ...

The Earth is a living being that existed long before humans did. It provides us with the soil that allows our food to grow. What do we do with the soil? We overuse it until it's almost sterile, then add artificial toxins called "fertilizers" that we think will substitute the natural ingredients that are missing, and so in the end the food that grows in it becomes a quality-lacking toxin itself. We collect such food, spray it with more toxins so it can live longer and look nicer when it gets to the stores weeks later. We cook it, killing the remains of any nutrition that was still left there, add poisons such as sugar, and eat it not thinking much of it. Then we get digestive problems and don't understand why we got sick and the medicines can't help us feel better.

The toxins in the ground spread to the underlying waters, which feed these poisons to the trees and plants until they start dying, unable to provide source of nourishment for the animals, birds, and other living beings so they too become sick and start to disappear from the face of the Earth. The sick trees cannot make as much oxygen as possible, especially that the air around them is so poisoned with fumes - the leftovers of our civilized lives. We breathe that impoverished air and wonder why we get lung cancer, even if we don't smoke cigarettes.

As the plants keep on dying, we find new and improved ways to make them (not grow them!), by adding other creatures' DNA to the fruits and vegetables, kill their natural defenses against those foreign agents with viruses, and end up with huge amounts of genetically modified foods that I'm not really sure are actually fruits and vegetables, or parts of animals too? Either we eat these food-like products, often packed in cans or boxes with added chemicals called "preservatives" or we feed them to the farm animals and then eat their meat that also carries the modified DNA. How do you think that modified, chemically filled food affects your own human DNA?

If that wasn't enough, cows, pigs, and chickens live in inhumane conditions to save the costs of keeping them and are continuously fed antibiotics to kill the numerous infections that arise in such environments. Did you know that there is a natural barrier that won't allow animal bacteria and viruses to attack human cells? Well, there used to be, as you're probably aware of the Avian Flu that killed many people not so long ago. Due to overuse of antibiotics, animal bacteria and viruses are able to pass that natural barrier and start affecting human beings too. Such infections cannot be treated with antibiotics, as the bacteria are already immune to them! And there are no cures for viral infections...

The toxins we use, not only in food industry, but also in factory productions of our civilization improvements, in cleaning chemicals, beauty products, not to mention radioactive plants and other 20th and 21st century inventions, travel through the Earth's soil deep into our sweet water supplies, poisoning the water we drink and then reach the rivers and oceans, killing the creatures that lived there since the beginning of time.

People kill animals in the name of sport, fun, material possessions, or to expand their lands of destruction. They disturb the gentle harmony of ecosystems where one animal is depended on other animal for survival, as in the ancient Wheel of Life structure. When the wolves are driven almost to starvation and attack humans to survive, people call them evil and feel justified to kill them almost to extinction.

The human nation is the race of waste. We produce more that we can consume and leave piles of rubbish as our legacy. Instead of reusing things, such as clothes, bottles, furniture, we throw them out and make more new ones, destroying the Earth and the air in the process and building more and more mountains of garbage that will stay there long after we and our children are gone.

There are more and more new diseases and illnesses that do not respond medical treatments, people are born with inner or outer mutations, and have immune systems of a premature infant. We suffer from chronic health conditions and die in pain and suffering. All that thanks to the way we treated that planet that gave us all we needed to survive and asked for nothing in return but respect. How is it possible not to see the connection between the planet and our lives?

You make your life choices, and what you do matters also to the Earth. Make the decision now to help this battered planet heal. Choose natural products that don't require chemicals in production process. Grow your own vegetables using natural fertilizers that actually allow the soil to gain in quality. Or support your local organic farmers and in turn enjoy healthier body. Recycle the packaging that comes with what you buy and don't buy more than you need. Reuse old clothes to make new ones or give them away to someone else who might need them. Carpool or use buses, or maybe just take a walk instead of driving yourself everywhere. Fewer fumes mean less pollution, cleaner air, and a healthier environment for everyone. Read and get informed on other ways you can support the healing process of our planet and make others aware of what is going on. There is an enormous power in awareness and one person *can* make a difference. Why can't it be you?

"The kindest thing you can do for yourself is to be the person that you would most like to spend the rest of your life with."
~ Heather K. O'Hara ~

Miracle of Choice

Mirjam looked at the sun setting behind the gentle waves of the ocean waters. Her road was bumpy, but she knew now that she was on the right path. If it wasn't for all that she'd been through, she would not be where she is now. If she hadn't made the choices she did, she would be someone else. And she didn't regret any of them. There were really no bad roads, just maybe less pleasant ones. But each turn she took, each road, street, and path brought her closer to discovering herself. Not the person she pretended to be so others liked her, but the real Mirjam, the one she forgot existed.

Lot of things happened since she chose to listen to her heart instead of letting unconscious forces decide for her. She went on adventures. She tried different professions. She lived in exotic countries. She met so many interesting people!

Mirjam got up from the rock she was sitting on and walked away slowly, conscious on her path now and determined to enjoy every minute of her journey, supported by never-ending Miracles of Choice.

11.

EPILOGUE

The concept of the "Power of Choice" been known since the 19th century when Frederick Bailes introduced it within his "Science of Mind" philosophy. But haven't we fought many wars throughout history to regain our freedom to choose what kind of lives we want to lead? The richest and most powerful of this world have been trying to force people into submission for centuries, depriving them from their right to free will but were never completely successful as people will not give up their most important God-given gift so easily.

In most countries, we now have that freedom to choose but we seemed to have forgotten that we once fought so fiercely to get it back. And what do we do with such power? We willingly give it away to our own insecurities, negative beliefs, and unprofitable habits. We give it away through being unaware of what we're doing and why we're doing it.

I hope that this book allowed you to see the amazing gifts that your own power choice gives you. Its "miracles" are the tools that you have to build your life with. I wanted to show you ways to claim back your true inner power, so that you can reach your highest potential and deepest fulfillment that you deserve. Now that you know what to do, don't go back to what you've been doing so far. Use this new knowledge and practice the skills until making positive choices for yourself becomes your newest, biggest, strongest habit. Use this knowledge and share it with others, so they too can learn to use their free will consciously for their benefit. Only by walking on our divine paths guided by Love, with an open hearth and hand in hand with the Miracles of Choice, we can make this world a better place for each and every one of us to live in.

～⊙⌇⟲⌇⊙～

"Man's power of choice enables him to think like an angel or a devil, a king or a slave. Whatever he chooses, mind will create and manifest"
~ Frederick Bailes ~

12.

INSPIRATIONS

I am not the first person to ever wonder about the meaning of life and how does this whole earthly existence works for a simple human being. While writing this book, I've received a lot of inspiration from the "Source Above", often sitting down to my laptop with empty head and nothing to go on with except this amazing deep feeling of excitement.

Some say that there is a plane around the Earth that is called Collective Consciousness, where all the thoughts of anyone who ever lived, lives, and will live reside. One may tap into that huge library of knowledge in the moments of peaceful openness to receive. I have a hunch that I was blessed with being able to access some of these thoughts. The others I've gathered in my mind through many books I've read and I would like to thank the authors for their amazing work. If you'd like to explore the subjects of subconsciousness, inner power, or the Law of Attraction, here's the list of the authors and books that made the biggest impact on my life and work. I hope that one day someone will mention *Miracles of Choice* on their list of inspirations.

With Love and Light,

Lorelai I. Dali

BIBLIOGRAPHY

Paulo Coelho - "The Alchemist"

Louise L. Hay - "You Can Heal Your Life"

Don Miguel Ruiz - "Four Agreements"

Colin C. Tipping - "Radical Forgiveness"

Abraham - Hicks - "Ask and it is Given"

Rhonda Byrne - "The Secret"

Byron Katie - "The Work"

Mike Dooley - "Infinite Possibilities"

... And many more ...

APPENDIX
~ Goal Spreadsheet ~

MY GOAL / DREAM: Positive, Personal, Present Tense
What will that do for you? In what way?
When do you want it? How long do you want it for?
Is what you want worth wanting? Why?
Is there any context in which you don't want it?
Is there anything you will lose as a result of this dream?
What stops you from reaching your dream/goal?
What have you been gaining out of this resistance?
Find 3 other ways to get this gain without resistance action/attitude 1._____ 2._____ 3._____
Create imaginary scene of already living your dream.
In what ways you can act 'as if'?

~ STOP Technique Spreadsheet ~

Stop	I feel:
Think	Why am I having this emotion, this feeling?
Situation Present	What is happening in my life right now that may cause this feeling?
	Is my emotional reaction proportionate to this situation?
	If this situation happened to someone else, would they have similar reaction or not?
	If my friend or family member reacted in this way to the same situation, what would I tell them?
No Situation Present	What is the thought behind this emotion?
	Is this thought actually true?
	What proofs do I have that it is true?
	What proofs do I have that it is not true?
	What positives is this thought bringing into my life?
	What negatives is this thought bringing into my life?
	How would I feel without this thought?
	Do I still want this thought?
Opt for Positive	What is the positive thought, opposite to what I was thinking thus far, that I may choose that will benefit my life?
	*How does this thought make me feel?

~ Ba-Gua Square ~

WEALTH & BLESSINGS	FAME	RELATIONSHIP & LOVE
FAMILY & HEALTH	CENTER	CHILDREN & CREATIVITY
KNOWLEGDE & SPIRITUALITY	CAREER	HELPFUL PEOPLE & TRAVEL

Ba-Gua Square

RELATIONSHIP & LOVE	FAME	WEALTH & BLESSINGS
CHILDREN & CREATIVITY	CENTER	FAMILY & HEALTH
HELPFUL PEOPLE & TRAVEL	CAREER	KNOWLEDGE & SPIRITUALITY